BEADS TO BUCKSKINS

BY
PEGGY SUE HENRY

This volume focuses on cradleboards, their construction and beadwork. Featuring full color photographs of antique cradleboards and newly constructed ones. Illustrated also are the side stitch weave (two versions), beaded boot tabs, beaded buckskin flowers, beaded button cover, beaded hair bun cover, garment decor with beads and a special eight pages of color patterns.

2 Timothy 2:19: God's solid foundation stands firm, sealed with this inscription, "The Lord knows those who are His," and, "Everyone who confesses the name of the Lord must turn away from wickedness.

Contents

Introduction

The center of our attention is on the cradleboards of the North American Indian in this volume. The cradleboard designs shown are of different tribes, primarily the plains or Mid-America regions. Certain structural styles were usually related to a specific tribe or nation. We have focused on beadwork as well as structural form to help identify the tribe or nation of origin.

Cradleboards serve a dual purpose. They shelter the child from the elements, while freeing the mothers hands for other chores. The cradleboards were sometimes tied into a tree, a safe distance up from the ground, to avoid predators and other dangers, while mother worked. The board was worn on mothers back while walking or riding a horse, much like the modern backpack. It kept the baby's back straight for health purposes and gave the baby a sense of security.

The headboard was not only used for shade, but protected the child from injury in case the board was dropped. Some of the southwestern styles have two pointed boards protruding from the top with a crown board around the head. If the cradle was dropped or fell from a horse the points would stick into the ground while the crown board protected the head and kept the baby's body from injury.

Indian women took great pride in their children. They decorated their clothes and cradleboard as elaborately as their bead supply would allow. The indian mother was responsible for the training of the boy child from infancy through primary age. Then the father or male relatives took over and manhood training began.

The girl child remained close to her mother and was trained in the ways of homemaking, which included beading, tanning, and making cradleboards.

Cradleboards were passed down from baby to baby and generation to generation. Some of the boards have beadwork that began in the early 1800's and was finished several children and decades later by new generations of mothers. The beadwork of others may not be aboriginal, but rather an imitation of a European design as glass beads found their way across the plains.

Little indian girls were trained for motherhood with dolls, just as little girls are today. Doll cradleboards were made and designed in detail exactly like the larger, real baby sizes.

In the color section of this volume, we show photographs of beaded doll cradleboards. The love and care that went into the making of these miniatures is obvious. The collectors of Native American items truly appreciate the beaded cradleboards.

Some indian mothers still use the boards for infants up to six months old. However, it is a classic tradition that is fading fast. The modern car seat, cribs, play pens, and backpacks for babies have replaced the cradleboards.

It is the intention of this author to instill a desire to create a cradleboard for your own collection. Discover new levels of creativity in beading as you begin a beautiful art form of the past. From inspiration to completion, you will enjoy constructing and beading a cradleboard. We, at "Beads to Buckskins", have gathered information and worked to make it easier for you with illustration and technique. We introduce you to work done by other beaders, generations ago, as well as today through photography. You may want to incorporate the help of a friend who understands working with wood for a cradleboard project. However, we will make it as easy as possible for you to understand the procedures. You will discover how beading with instructions that show how a little spontaneity can help you create color combinations and visual patterns you only dreamed of before. If you are like many beaders, you know that patterns are an essential part of beading. You can learn to design with bead graph paper and develop skills to open up endless possibilities in your beading artistry and free

you forever from the limitations of ready made patterns. Every beginner can create gorgeous heirlooms. Some of the brightest and best new ideas come from the beginner. You will enjoy adding your own decorative touch, simply, easily, and beautifully. With beads, you can create everything from a decorative cradleboard to festive Christmas ornaments, or perhaps a special gift for a special friend. Beads express love for a lifetime.

This series of books has special sections that offers numerous tips on how to make the construction faster and easier. Details that make a big difference in how your finished product looks and marketing ideas. Regardless, if you are a bead enthusiast or someone who has never considered beading, this series will help develop your interests and change the way you look at this classic craft.

You will find easy to follow illustrated instructions, helpful hints and full color photographs. You will get all the inspiration and know-how you need to create your own treasured and admired beadwork. Discover dozens of ways to use beads to create stunning designs from combination techniques and color into sensational finished products. The timeless art of beading can give you the ultimate self-satisfaction. We at "Beads to Buckskins" don't claim to know it all, however, we are willing to share the knowledge we have with others. Happy Beading!!!

Acknowledgements

A special thanks goes out to the following people for their contribution of photographs and sharing their beading talents with us: Custer Battlefield Trading Post, Crow Agency, Montana, The Hastings Museum, Hastings, Nebraska, Doris Barnes, Tommie Prentice, Creative Corner in Miami, Oklahoma, Dawna Jolliff, Emma Copeland, Mary Wagon, Jude Biegert of Bead Lady Designs, Melody Abbott, Sioux Trading Post in Rapid City, SD, Jennifer Tallbear, Lois McCoy, Tandy Leather, Redding, CA, RT Computer Graphics and many others who have shared their beadwork in photo with us. We appreciate all the hard work and dedication you contribute to your craft.

We continue to endeavor into new avenues concerning this series, I would like to thank my husband, Richard Henry and my secretary, Denise Babcock for all their help, support, and patience in producing these volumes.

The instructional illustrations and patterns in this volume were done by the author. As for the patterns used by the beaders in the photo sections of this and all volumes of "Beads to Buckskins", I can not be responsible. Their original origin is not known to me and my only interest is showing the finished products of beadwork of other people, not publishing the pattern of that particular beadwork.

There are other techniques not shown in this volume that have been illustrated in the first seven volumes: loom beading, split loom necklace illustrations, overlay or applique stitch, edge or fret stitching, lazy stitch, brick-stitch earring and patterns, spanish lace earrings, cradleboard earrings, peyote stitch, daisy chain, indian flower chevron, moccasin and buckskin shirt and squaw dress, peyote stitch (new method), beaded belt buckles, hair ornaments, brain tanning method, loom beading without-a-loom, cabochon jewelry instructions, beaded fringe, "best kept secrets", off-loom weaving, quill work, tambour beading, tribal color identity, navajo loose weave necklace and earring techniques, marketing tips. Combined volumes give your over 1400 patterns.

We have a store source list available to help find beads and beading supplies from areas all over the United States. The wooden loom illustrated in the first three volumes, the big eye needle, and the tambour needle and book wholesale price list are available through the publishers address on the back. Send a self-addressed stamped envelope to the address on the back of this book with a not requesting a store and source list.

About the Author

Those of us who love beading and crafts, seem always to be searching for the ultimate, highest achievement that can be attained, however impossible it may seem. I have discovered that the ultimate is imply "more of it" and the highest achievement "is finishing the project started". I tend to start more projects than I can possibly finish in the time I have allotted. Overextending myself is practically habit. To break the habit, I keep forcing myself to finish one project before beginning another. And, if the idea for a new one pops through my mind, I write it down for a later date, rather than start it right then. If all this sounds familiar to you, then I welcome you to what I refer to as "bead fever".

Throughout this series, I have tried to emphasize how beading can act as a stress reliever and help to relieve tension and control anxiety. Keeping your hands and mind busy and concentrating on any needle or other craft will probably do the same. However, I prefer beading. You don't have to prove yourself to anybody. Just self-satisfaction of achievement will do it. Beading has a way of taking your mind off all the surrounding events that are happening and leaves no room to worry about them. When I sit down in my easy chair and pick up my beading, the busy world stops and my creative, relaxing world begins. If you have a studio or craft room to work in, it's even more relaxing because you can separate yourself from the rest of the household and concentrate better.

I have researched beadwork of the Native American Indian for a lot of years and the longer I search, the more I realize what talented ancestors many of us had. One of the things that amazes me most are the primitive tools and materials these people had to work with, yet they created such beautiful things. When we consider most of the delicate beadwork had to be done during the daylight hours along with all the other daily necessary preparations for feeding the family, gathering wood, tanning skins, and literally, making a comfortable home for their family, plus many other duties. The Native American Indian women would find time to bead or quill. I feel certain that this must have been when their relaxing world began also.

As you admire the beautifully beaded craddleboards in this volume, keep in mind the love and compassion the women who made them must have had for their children. And how privileged we are that they left us a great legacy.

Marketing Tips

For the crafter who has unanswered questions concerning a home based business, I recommend the following book for helpful suggestions on beginning your own business. An excerpt from "Homemade Success in a Home based Business" (Betterway Publication) copyright 1992 by Barbara Brabec. Reprinted by permission. The 1992 4th Revised Edition of this home business classic includes detailed guidance on how to successfully start, manage and market a home based business. (All tax and legal information has been verified for accuracy by attorneys and other business specialists.) "Homemade Money" is available by mail for $21.95 ppd. from Barbara Brabec Productions, P. O. Box 2137, Naperville, IL 60567. The author's Home Business Success Catalog" is free on request. The updated fifth edition is to be released in March, 1994.

Another book just off the press that will help you with ordering supplies and understanding the terms used in beading while adding a little humor with cute cliques is called "Bead Talk" by Shirley Worley and Peggy Crisman. I recommend this adorable little book for anyone interested in beading. It can be purchased through Beads Unique, 308 Roberts Lane, Bakersfield, California 93308.

To get acquainted with the bead-work market, you should first familiarize yourself with the different markets that are available in your area (local craft shows, fairs, etc).

The Native American Pow Wow is a learning experience for all beadwork crafters. I recommend the Whispering Wind Magazine as a source for keeping in touch with the Native American movement and pow wow calenders. For information write: Whispering Wind Magazine, 8009 Wales Street, New Orleans, Louisiana 70126-1952.

Pow wow's take place all over the United States and Canada during spring, summer and fall and most have craft booths available to venders who sell related items pertaining to the Native American.

If the pow wow is held on a reservation, you will probably have to apply for a license or permit to sell on that particular reservation. I'm sure you will agree that it is worth it all. You will find that the Native American people appreciate your efforts to bring your crafts and materials to them. And if you do their craft shows and pow wow's regularly, they extend their friendship and wait for you to come, before buying from someone else.

Speaking as a Native American, If our world leaders could get along as well as the many nations of Native Americans at an inner tribal pow wow, it would be a much better world to live.

Many pow wow's include peoples that are not of Native American heritage in the ceremonies. I'm not suggesting that each event is a free-for-all. Rather, a well organized celebration of tradition enjoyed by all peoples. So check the pow wow calenders for events near you and become involved with a special, exciting, heart-warming people.

For help in establishing a home craft business. I recommend that you become a member of The Craft Center, a non-profit, membership organization. The center serves the interest and needs of low income artisans by providing technical assistance and information to help artisans achieve markets to sell your crafts. Need help in starting your own business? Looking for sources for low-cost credit? Craft Center members can receive information on groups, organizations, and individuals which provide information in these, and more craft areas. Members also receive "Craft News"; a quarterly newsletter which is a source of information on crafts activities worldwide, and "Development and Marketing Manual". Membership dues are $35 annually for artisans. For further information, please write: The Craft Center, Membership Director, 1001 Connecticut Avenue, N. W., Suite 1138, Washington, D. C. 20036.

It 's very difficult to sell your crafts from home without a catalog or portfolio to help describe your work. Presentation of the craft items is a large part of sales. Keep in mind the pattern used. If you are using a pattern from a craft book to construct your products, you must keep it on a personal retail level. For wholesale, you will need permission from the person or publisher that owns the copyrights of that pattern. Barbara Brabec's book will answer questions to help you understand copyrights.

When you print a catalog, it should be of patterns you have designed yourself. A catalog is a publication and might be infringing on copyrights.

Wearable art can be a very profitable business. Consumers appreciate "one-of-a-kind items" and the beader can capitalize on any hand beaded apparel. If you are a sports fan, support your local football or sports team by creating gift items in the team colors. Our home team displays red, white, and black on their uniforms. Some local crafters make wearable items in those colors such as beaded earrings, necklaces, belts, hat bands with teams name in the beadwork. Bracelets, hand bags, tot bags, beaded socks, beaded hair ribbons or any apparel that can be displayed to support their team. A crafty minded beader can capitalize on this trend and stay buzy. Expand your personalized craft business by including the team colors of the neighboring towns.

Constructing Cradleboards

Like many crafters, especially leather craft persons, you may have already tried your hand at some basic beading techniques. But, perhaps you have shied away from intricate or large scale projects because you lack the skill or time required to complete them. In this chapter, we show you easy ways to convert your ambitions to real hands on accomplishments you can cherish for a lifetime.

Cradleboards are a massive project and look very complicated. Actually they are basically simple to construct. It would be a good idea to begin constructing a doll or small size cradleboard first. You will get a better understanding of the basic principals involved in constructing a full sized cradleboard without using a lot of materials. It's the beadwork that takes the time. We will show you beading short cuts and explain how to apply them for the best results.

The inner structure of a cradleboard is usually made of a sturdy, lightweight wood or basketry of woven wickerwork as a base. The Umatilla Indians of Oregon were great basket weavers. Many other nations mastered the art. The origin of the basket maker indians is not precisely known, however the title "Basket Maker" has been applied to the Pueblo Indian known the world over for their beautiful basketry.

It was not unusual to see basket head shades attached to wooden framed cradleboards from east to west coasts. Although the classic cradleboard designs are basic and simple, they still offer a creative challenge. Their beautiful beadwork arrangements has warmed hearts for decades.

Appliqued beadwork is used on a lot of cradleboards. You can cover a lot of area very fast using the lane (lazy) stitch and a size 11/o bead. For a floral design, I use the applique technique and for geometric, the lane stitch. You can combine the two techniques and add others. Loomed strips work well on the sides or body area of the baby wrap. Combining different techniques into a project helps to break up the boredom of repetitive movements. They also add a flair of beading talents incorporated into one project. You can work with the wonderful assortment of cross stitch patterns and iron on transfer patterns for quick results. All of the enchanting ideas going through your mind are just waiting for your hands to bring them to life and worth every minute of the time you spend making them. Throughout the country, thousands of people like you are continuing the traditions of beading and contributing to its future. Don't be too concerned about two needle beadwork techniques. If it's easier for you, then use them. However, most beaders find the single needle, single thread for overlay is much easier and quicker, although the single thread is sometimes referred to as the "white mans technique". If we had to be really authentic, we would be using sinew instead of the wonderful modern nylon and acrylic threads available to us today. When the project is finished, it will look just as good done with single thread and needle as the traditional two needle technique. However, if you are repairing old beadwork, I suggest you use the original technique.

To begin construction of a cradleboard, you must first decide on style. You will need these materials: #1-wood for frame (preferably cedar) 32" by 16" by 1/2 thick. #2-Buckskin or soft leather for covering; 30 square feet will cover the back and front, and have enough left over for the straps, fringe and laces. Blanket cloth can be used in place of leather #3-leather glue, #4-leather punch, #5-scissors, #6-tailors cloth measuring tape, #7-tracing wheel, #8-small nails with large head, #9-sandpaper, #10-glover or leather needles size 3 to 5, #11-waxed sinew, #12-beadwork is optional. For materials needed for beadwork, refer to "Choosing the Right Materials" on page (#68) in this volume.

The following pages give four basic examples of styles. Cedar is flexible, yet strong, while at the same time pre-

vents moths and bugs from destroying the leather and fabric materials used. The dimensions vary, depending on age limit of the child. Most boards carry infants up to seven months. The height (top to bottom) of the average cradleboard is 2 1/2 to 3 feet. Measurements for the solid board framed cradleboard are shown in plate # 5. The width across the circumference of the bow at the base of the half circle is 15 1/2". Across the bottom, the frame measures 7 1/2".

It isn't necessary to use a thick board. Less than 1/2" thick is preferred. You don't want the added weight. Make a pattern of preferred size of inner board before cutting. Newspaper works well. Next trace around the pattern onto the board.

If you are like me, using a saw of any kind is all Greek. So, after I trace the pattern onto the wood, I take it to the nearest lumber yard, carpenter or high school wood shop and pay them to cut it out the right way for me. If your talents include using a jig saw, you are lucky.

You will also need to drill two lines of holes along each side of the baby body area, large enough to feed several inches long and one inch wide. (Hole pattern illustrated Plate # 5).

The same hole pattern is used to attach the buckskin cover to the bottom half or body area of the cradleboard and secure the baby. The lace will prevent the infant from slipping from side to side in the cradle wrap. The two holes on each side of the head area can be used for attaching backpack straps and head canopy.

Some head canopies are a piece of leather or fabric arranged around the baby's head, much as a hood might be on a coat, then tacked into place using small nails with large heads.

The Navajo used a sheepskin with wool on, as a pad for the child's back and a hand woven rug draped over the canopy board for shade and warmth.

Since the headboard is flat and the buckskin is permanently attached, you must do the beadwork and attach it to the buckskin before assembling.

You can do the beadwork on fabric or leather and applique the finished beadwork to the buckskin cover or you can do the beadwork directly on the cover. Remember to allow space for the hood attachment. I find it easier and time saving to do the beadwork separately, then applique it on with an edge stitch. For a different and unique look, you can inlay the finished bead-work, framing all around the edge with a leather laced, herring bone stitch, rather than appliqueing it on.

When you have your beadwork in place and you have given thought to how you want to use the extra buckskin around the pattern, then you are ready to assemble the cradleboard.

1. Carefully sandpaper all the sawed edges of the wooden frame smooth. Any rough places will cause the leather to wear.

2. If you have decided not to fringe around the top, cut the buckskin headboard pattern out, leaving one inch on the outside of the traced line.

3. Back cover: Using the paper pattern, trace and cut buckskin for the back cover of the cradleboard (allow one inch seam).If the leather is large enough, cut the back pattern in one piece.

Now you have an option. One,you can glue the top-front and back cover to the board and use tacks or nails all the way around the edge, lapping the front seam over the back. The fringe will be cut to cover the nails. Two, for a more finished look, I prefer lacing or sewing the front and back cover seams together with leather or sinew. Then fitting the cover over the top, much like fitting a pillowcase on a pillow. Glue the top cover in place to prevent slipping and stretching the leather while working on the bottom half.

4. Now that you have the top half of the cradleboard covered, you have some options on covering the bottom half.

First I will explain the methods I use to work the leather into place.Then I will explain some traditional ways used by many of the Plains Indians in covering a cradleboard with buckskin or blanket cloth.

I like the look of fringe hanging around the bottom half. To allow the fringe to be connected to the front cover, I cut the back cover to pattern size, allowing a 1/2" seam. If you have cut the complete back pattern in one piece, all the better. Glue and attach the back cover in place (do not glue the front bottom half). Tuck and glue the back cover seam around the edge of the wooden frame. Tap the glued seam gently with a rawhide or wooden mallet to flatten the tucks into place.

5. Attach the front cover by lapping and gluing the traced pattern seam only, over the edge, covering the seam of the back cover. Make no cuts in the front cover yet. When you have glued the seam and gently tapped with mallet to seal, allow glue to dry completely. If you have decided you don't care to fringe around the bottom or add some beadwork to the extra leather. Trim the excess leather now. The edge seam must be secured with more than glue. You can easily secure the seams by sewing with sinew and leather needle, using the whip stitch all the way around the bottom edge.

If you prefer, tack the seam down with small nails. I have seen spacer beads used with the nails as a flat washer would be used with a bolt. The nail head holds the bead on. Brass or other metal beads work well.

6. When you have secured the edge seam, locate the lines of drilled holes in the wooden frame, front and back, by feeling. Lightly mark each one with a lead pencil.

With a tracing wheel, trace a vertical line on each side of the front center line, from shoulder to foot, one inch from the center. Now you may cut the front center line. Cut the center line from the bottom seam through the top of the skin. Do not cut through the bottom glued and secured seam (refer to plate #7). Allow the extra leather above the shoulder line to fold back toward the bottom of the board, as a collar would fold. Using the two vertical traced lines for a guide, punch an equal amount of holes along each side of the center seam opening from the shoulder line to foot. These holes are for lacing the front together, as you would lace a shoe. The holes should be one inch away from the cut seam.

Use a mallet and single punch to make holes large enough for a lace one inch wide to pass through or cut small slits(using a single edge razor blade) in the buckskin at each drilled hole you marked with a pencil. If the leather lifts away from the wood, you may want to re-glue around the back holes by applying glue in small amounts with a glue brush through the holes.

The front cover is loose so you should be able to punch the marked holes easier.

8. Cut two buckskin laces one inch wide by 20" long. (# 23 plate) These laces will hold the baby's body in place. Lace each side separately. Begin threading the buckskin lace at the top hole.Passing through the drilled holes and both front and back covers (see illustration, # 20 plate). leave a ten

inch tail of lace at the starting hole to tie off later. Leave remaining lace at bottom or last hole.

#9. Cut small lacing 1/3" wide and two yards long. (illustrated plate # 23) Begin lacing from the bottom, center opening and cross lace to top hole. (Like lacing a shoe)

#10. You can add beadwork to the edge of the fold back buckskin on the shoulder line or cut into fringe. **Cut the fringe after the glue dries and all the beading details are completed.** If you cut the fringe before completing all other details, you will have a lot of leather strings in the way.

The traditional way of covering a cradle board varies from tribe to tribe. Some tribes used blanket cloth while others used what ever materials were available. Soft leather or buckskin was most frequently used in areas where game was abundant.

Some of the Ute cradleboards were covered by wrapping a large buckskin over the front. Covering the front completely, leaving the opening on the backside to be closed by lacing together. Then cutting a hole across the front for the basket, head canopy, to be connected.

Allowing enough slack around the body area for the baby, they cut a vertical center line and laced the front together. To hold the baby in place, the body area was attached to the frame on each side and under the feet with leather lacing. A leather strip was laced in place across the chest on the outside of the cover.

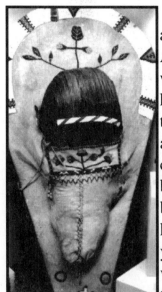

Ute Cradleboard was made in the middle 1800's.

Most of the antique Native American beadwork we see today has been preserved through museums and special private collections. The beaded cradleboards seem to have weathered the years very well, which indicates that they have always been a prized possession. The beadwork was not always done on leather as the Nez Perse cradleboard shows,(pictured in this chapter). So if you don't have leather available , you can still construct an authentic looking cradle using blanket cloth.

Nez Perse Indian Cradleboard which has been appliqued on blanket cloth with buckskin at bottom. Made in middle 1800's. Courtesy of The Hastings Museum, Hastings, Nebraska.

The Cradleboard pictured with fully beaded top and pouch type baby carrier shows no leather at all. If not for the basic frame construction and beadwork patterns done on most cradleboards the identity of tribe and origin becomes almost impossible.

Solid frame cradleboard with fully beaded top over a pouch infant styled carrier. Cover is made of blanket cloth. Northern Colorado area, Plains Indians.

To construct a split framed cradleboard, as shown in plate # 2, you can use the same dimensions given for Navajo split cedar cradleboard, omitting the canopy and footboard.

The beadwork is done while the cover is flat and before the back piece of leather is sewn in. You will need to make a paper pattern to be sure you have the dimensions of the cradle cover right. The top of the hood will be the widest area.

In this volume, I show a very special loom beaded strip for a cradleboard done by Melody Abbott (see page 67). You can loom a cover in strips or square sections. You may want to applique the main body area and do some loomed strips to break up the pattern. There are many different ways to use separate beading techniques for a unique design on a cradle. It isn't necessary to bead a pattern solid or filled in completely with beads. Applique an outline of beads for a quick and easy pattern. A flower or animal outlined with beads still catching the eye. Color the body of the pattern with felt pens, or use colored felt for the pattern and do an edge stitch around it.

To make a miniature pattern this style for a doll cradleboard, I used the insole of a shoe for size on the back of the pattern, squaring the toe off and strengthening the side lines. (see # 21 plate). Then, I measured the circumference around the back pattern and cut a paper strip that length, five inches wide. Next, I tapered the strip to three inches at the bottom, by folding it in half and trimming two inches, tapering up to the elbow area. It made the hood area five inches deep and the foot area three inches deep when assembled. (see illustration, plate # 20). Next, I laid the strip of paper on leather and traced around it and the back pattern with a tracing wheel.

To add a finished decor to the front, lace loops of buckskin on each side of the center opening (body area--illustration plate # 24), then add crow beads to the ends of the extra lacing.

After completing the flat work, connect the back and body pieces. Begin sewing with the loop stitch at the top center and sew one side to center bottom. Then sew other side from top center to bottom. You may want to baste a temporary stitch every three inches to hold in place to avoid stretching. (Imagine how a shoe top is connected to the sole and use the same

Beaded Doll Cradleboard

application.)

There are several ways of connecting the beaded baby cover to the frame. You can attach buckskin tie-on's to each side and top. Or sew two leather loops across the back to slip over the frame points. Many of these beautifully beaded body blankets were not permanently attached to the frame. And some were not designed to be on a frame at all, but carried in the mother's arms. A cross bar of wood behind the head and at the foot, was sometimes used to brace the two vertical frame pieces together and the beaded cover was attached with leather ties.

To attach a basket canopy to the frame. Use a strip of leather three inches wide, long enough to reach across basket weave. Tack the basket into

place with small nails. Then place the leather strip across the weave, covering the edge of the weave. Use a little leather glue to hold into place. Secure the leather strip and weave using small nails with large heads , 1/2 inch apart, around the circumference of the leather.

Sioux Indian Doll made in 1875. Photograph courtesy of the The Hastings Museum, Hastings, Nebraska.

Sioux Buckskin Doll, The Hastings Museum, Hastings, Nebraska.

Antique Toy Cradleboards

All Photographs Courtesy of Custer Battlefield Trading Post, Crow Agency, Montana

Very old board based cradleboard. Early 1800's.

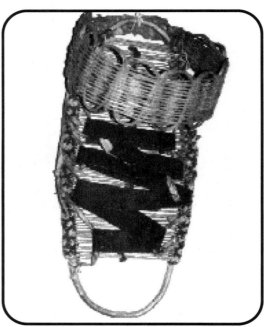

Basket weave cradleboard. Late 1800's.

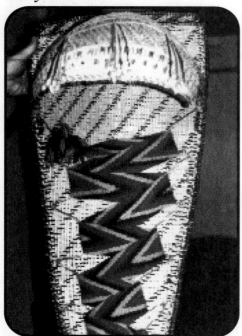

Beautifully woven reed cradleboard with basket crown and handwoven sash.

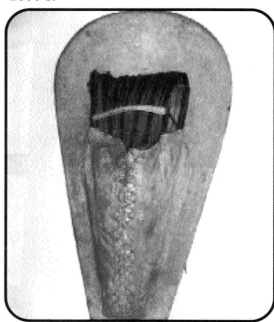

Buckskin covered cradleboard with woven reed head protection. Northern Plains--1800's.

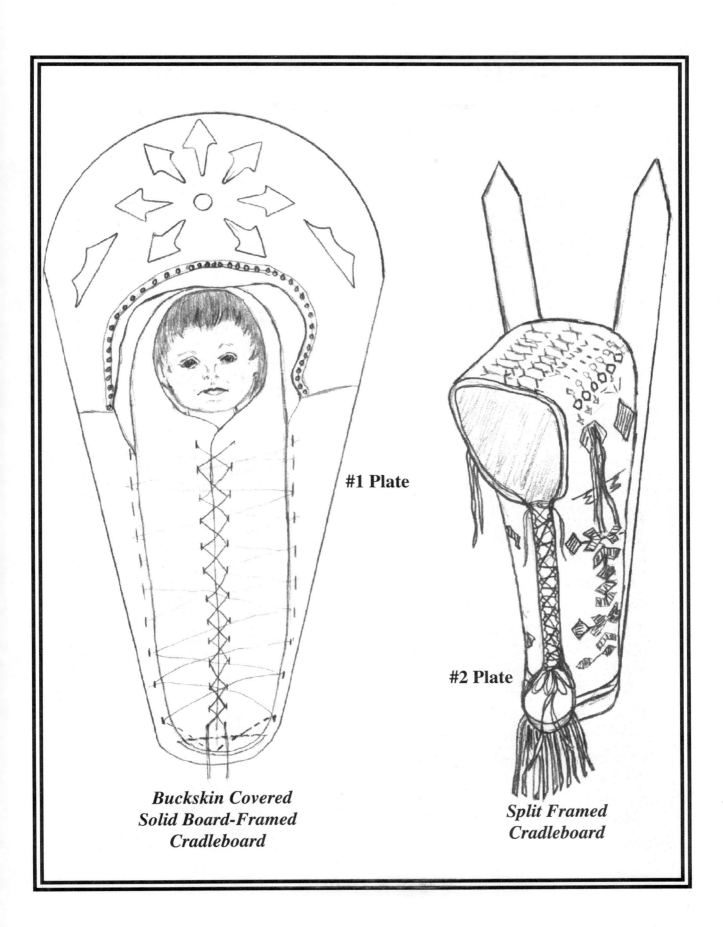

#1 Plate

#2 Plate

Buckskin Covered
Solid Board-Framed
Cradleboard

Split Framed
Cradleboard

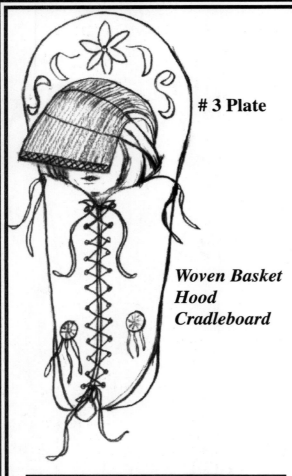

 # 3 Plate

Woven Basket Hood Cradleboard

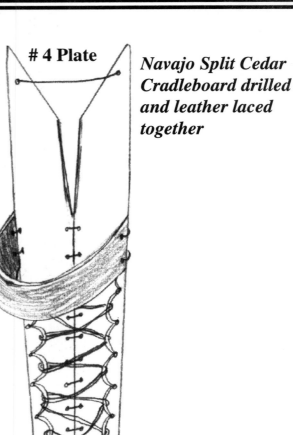

 # 4 Plate

Navajo Split Cedar Cradleboard drilled and leather laced together

The inside frame of the basket hood cradleboard is usually woven wicker also. However, the hood can be attached to a wooden frame. It's important that the attachment is not made behind the head area, but four to five inches above where the head lies. A split is made across the buckskin cover for the head basket to go through, then the buckskin is glued and attached securely to cover the basket attachment.

The split cedar is made of four pieces of wood. Two long, pointed pieces, 30 inches long graduating from 15 1/2" top to 7 1/2" bottom. One, 30" long by 3" wide for bow of the head canopy. To form bow, soak canopy board in water. Gradually bend to bow. Secure bowed position and allow to dry. One piece 6" x 3" for the support of the feet. All pieces are drilled and laced together with leather.

Preparing Leather for Beadwork

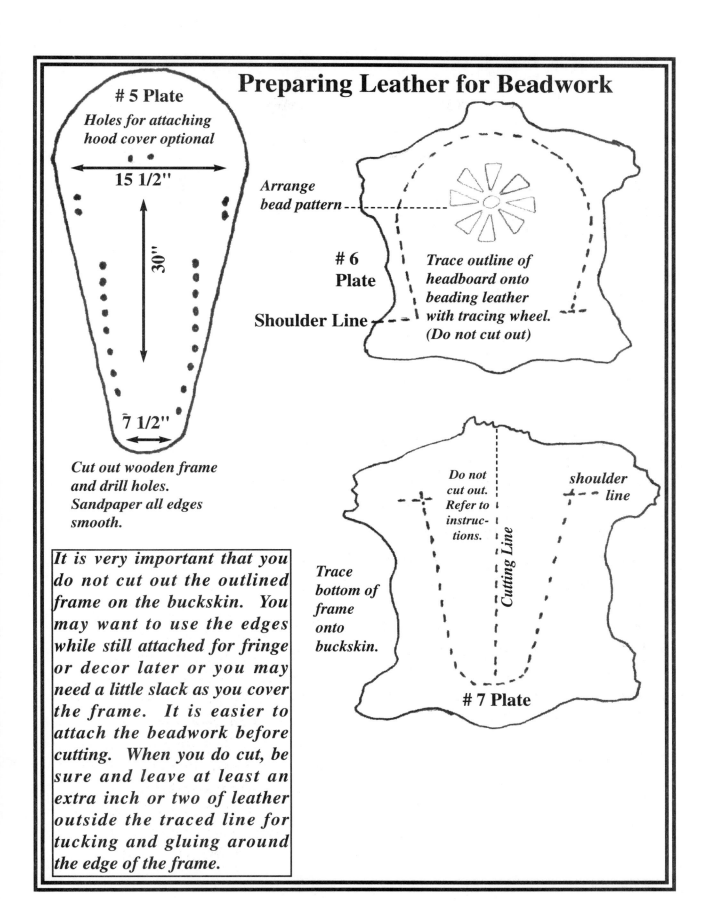

 # 5 Plate

Holes for attaching hood cover optional

15 1/2"

30"

7 1/2"

Cut out wooden frame and drill holes. Sandpaper all edges smooth.

Arrange bead pattern

 # 6 Plate

Shoulder Line

Trace outline of headboard onto beading leather with tracing wheel. (Do not cut out)

It is very important that you do not cut out the outlined frame on the buckskin. You may want to use the edges while still attached for fringe or decor later or you may need a little slack as you cover the frame. It is easier to attach the beadwork before cutting. When you do cut, be sure and leave at least an extra inch or two of leather outside the traced line for tucking and gluing around the edge of the frame.

Trace bottom of frame onto buckskin.

Do not cut out. Refer to instructions.

shoulder line

Cutting Line

 # 7 Plate

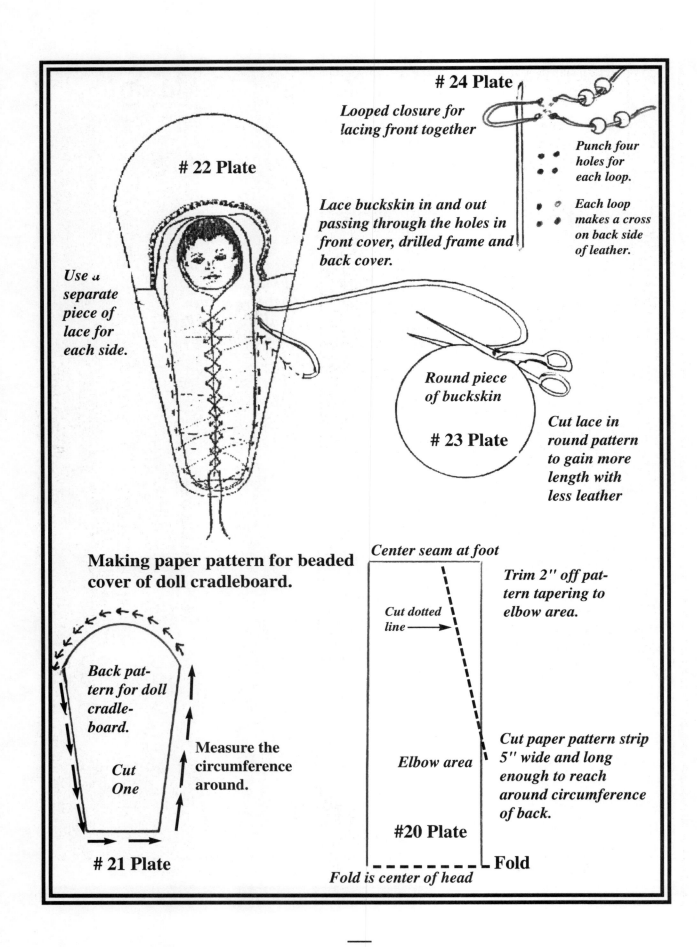

 # 24 Plate

Looped closure for lacing front together

Punch four holes for each loop.

Each loop makes a cross on back side of leather.

 # 22 Plate

Lace buckskin in and out passing through the holes in front cover, drilled frame and back cover.

Use a separate piece of lace for each side.

Round piece of buckskin

 # 23 Plate

Cut lace in round pattern to gain more length with less leather

Making paper pattern for beaded cover of doll cradleboard.

Center seam at foot

Trim 2" off pattern tapering to elbow area.

Cut dotted line →

Back pattern for doll cradleboard.

Cut One

Measure the circumference around.

Elbow area

Cut paper pattern strip 5" wide and long enough to reach around circumference of back.

 # 21 Plate

#20 Plate

Fold is center of head

— **Fold**

Ute style cradle made by Dawna Joliff. Shown in color section.

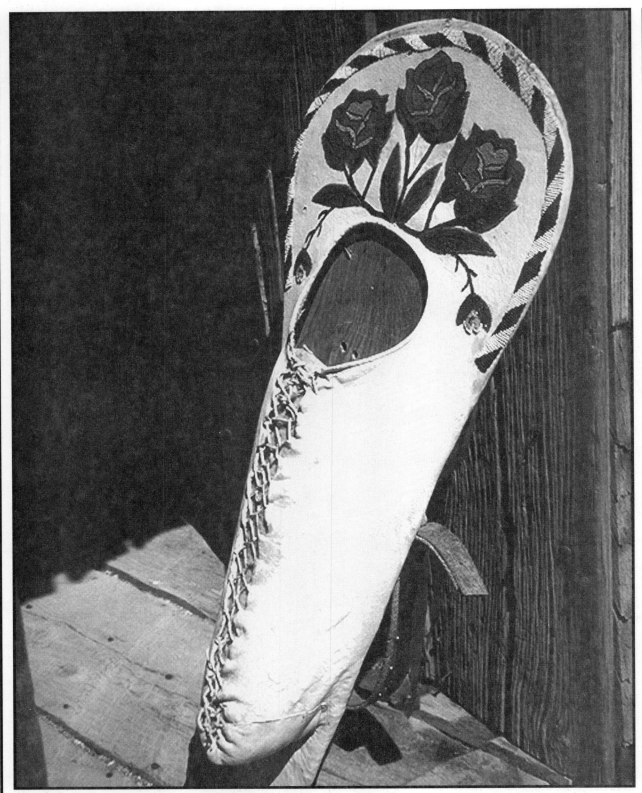

Shoshone cradle, 1915 from West Yellowstone, Montana. Maker, Mary Wagon. Shown in color section.

Northern Paiute/Shoshone cradle from Walker Lake, Nevada. Maker, Emma Copeland. Private Collection. Shown in color section.

Warm Springs cradle from Warm Springs, Oregon. Maker unknown. Private Collection. Shown in color section.

Beaded Hair Bun Covers

Sterling silver hair bun covers are very popular and expensive. As an alternative, we illustrate how to make a beaded hair bun cover.

These delightful, decorative hair ornaments are a refreshing change from barrettes and clip-on hair pieces. They will enhance your wardrobe and add another exotic beading technique to your own beading skills.

As you get into these hair pieces, they spark your imagination and open exciting new pattern variations and possibilities of creativity. You can take your beading skills to a new level of proficiency and create the kind of heirloom quality beadwork you have always wanted to make.

Most beaders began beading by making the brickstitch earrings (refer to Volume 1 for the brickstitch instruction). If you have that technique mastered, you can incorporate the brickstitched diamonds into this hair bun. Each diamond makes a petal or star point. The loom beading without a loom technique (illustrated in Volume 3) can also be used for the diamond (see plate #25).

Step 1. For the top of the hair bun, you will need to make five diamonds.

Step 2. Lay the five diamonds in a star pattern and connect the sections from the center to inset point of the star with needle and thread.

Step 3. Make a single fringe row, two inches long and connect at inset point of the star. There will be five fringes; one at each inset.

Step 4. To complete the webbing, string a single strand of beads long enough to reach from the star point to the fringe at the third bead up from the turn bead (illustrated as step #4) The bead count varies with size of beads used. However, each fringe should have the same count and each connecting section of single strand beads between the star point and the fringe should have the same count.

Step 5. After you have completed connecting the star points and fringes around the center piece, make a four bead fringe at each star point.

Step 6. Using elastic metallic thread and a size 10/o or larger seed bead, edge stitch around an elastic ponytail band. Allow as much stretching ease as possible in your elastic metallic thread. You will need twenty edge beads minimum. (illustrated as step #6)

Step 7. There should be ten, four bead fringes attached to the star. Connect the four bead fringes individually. One to every other edge bead on the elastic ponytail band.

If you don't feel comfortable using a ponytail band for this project, you can use a piece of buckskin lace and tie the bun on, leaving the lace ends hanging, decorated with larger beads.

To connect the star to the buckskin lace, you do the same edge stitch using regular beading thread on the lace. Leave a 10" tail of lace on each side of the edge beading for tying the bun on. For a larger bun, increase the bead count on the four bead fringes.

An appliqued rosette makes a beautiful center for a beaded hair bun. Use the same basic steps for webbing and edging as illustrated for the star bun.

Photograph is of the petal arrangements for the hair bun. These particular pieces are shown as flowers on a sweater. They can be used in so many different ways from moccasin toes to hair buns.

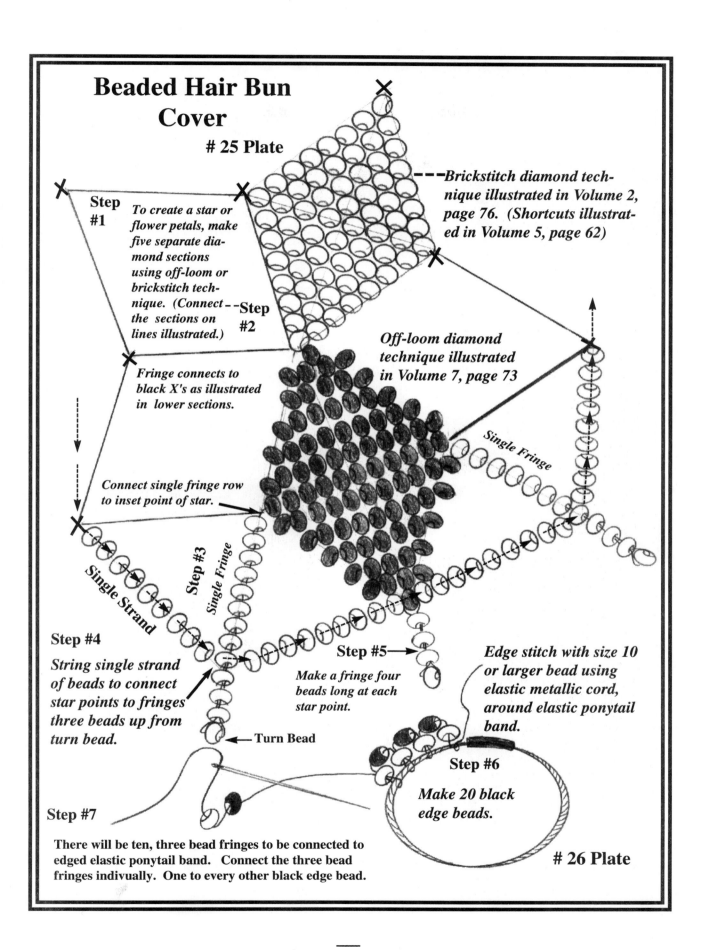

Beaded Hair Bun Cover

25 Plate

Step #1

To create a star or flower petals, make five separate diamond sections using off-loom or brickstitch technique. (Connect the sections on lines illustrated.)

Step #2

Fringe connects to black X's as illustrated in lower sections.

- - -*Brickstitch diamond technique illustrated in Volume 2, page 76. (Shortcuts illustrated in Volume 5, page 62)*

Off-loom diamond technique illustrated in Volume 7, page 73

Single Fringe

Connect single fringe row to inset point of star.

Single Fringe

Single Strand

Step #3

Step #4

String single strand of beads to connect star points to fringes three beads up from turn bead.

Step #5→

Make a fringe four beads long at each star point.

Edge stitch with size 10 or larger bead using elastic metallic cord, around elastic ponytail band.

←— **Turn Bead**

Step #6

Make 20 black edge beads.

Step #7

There will be ten, three bead fringes to be connected to edged elastic ponytail band. Connect the three bead fringes indivaully. One to every other black edge bead.

26 Plate

This white buckskin shirt has been bead in bold red, blue, yellow, brown, white. It is beautiful! Courtesy of Custer Battlefield Trading Post, Crow Agency, Montana.

Beaded flowers in red, yellow, and mauve have been appliqued on to the back of this handsome white buckskins jacket. Custer Battlefield Trading Post.

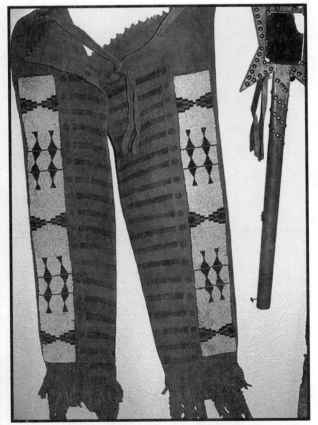

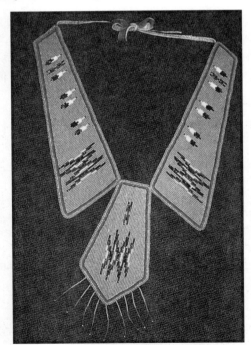

Buckskin male leggings. Beaded on the each side in natural colors. On display at Custer Battlefield Trading Post, Crow Agency, Montana.

This beautiful red, white, and blue collar and tie was used for special meeting occassions. Courtesy of Custer Battlefield Trading Post.

Side Stitch Weave

This technique produces a totally different look in beadwork. The slant of the beads make it very confusing for designing pattern. Once you get a picture in mind of how the direction of the geometrics work in the pattern, you realize it's like a diagonal basket weave. If you are a person who likes to macrame, this technique presents little challenge, other than the size of threads used.

The loom graph paper can be used for designing the diagonal weave. However, I prefer the honeycomb graph introduced in this series as brick and peyote graph. You get a better prospective of the finished look. The beads are woven across the pattern, but hang on a slant, similar to the peyote stitch slant. Example graphs are illustrated below.

I prefer using the Kevlar bead cord for this technique. You have to handle each warp and weft strands frequently and the Kevlar thread is very strong. It has a firm, yet flexible body that needs now wax to prevent becoming entangled. I've used this thread with the size 14/o Japanese bead successfully. You will need to wax the nymo beading thread.

The side stitch was used by the indians around the Great Lakes and northern plains areas. Finger weaving has become almost a lost art. It's a difficult technique to teach. However, once you get the basics down, you will enjoy creating the traditional ornaments of that period.

I didn't master this weave until twelve years ago and my understanding of it has a few modern shortcuts, because that is the way I learned. I will

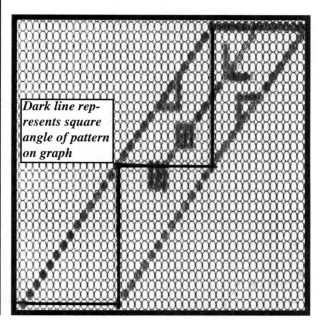

Dark line represents square angle of pattern on graph

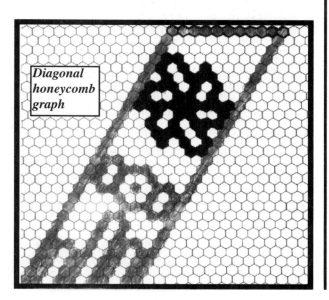

Diagonal honeycomb graph

also illustrate how to achieve the side stitch look with a single needle and thread.

It will be difficult to refer to weft and warp strands in these instructions, because each set of threads will pass through beads at one point making it the weft thread. The same set of threads will go between the beads at another point, making it the warp threads. So rather than trying to explain the differences, I have illustrated the moves in this technique as we go to avoid confusion. You may want to practice this technique with large crow bead and waxed sinew for a better understanding. Once you have completed a few rows, it becomes easier.

The traditional way of beginning the side weave:

1. Use soft leather or buckskin as anchor to attach the warp strands. Cut the leather across at a diagonal angle. (See plate # 8) You will need four times as much thread as the length of your beadwork for each double warp. Example: for a bead strip 1" wide by 4 1/2" long, the warp threads should be 18" long. Each warp thread is doubled, leaving the needle attached and hanging down. (See plate # 8) Connect the warps to the buckskin, using two embroider chain stitches. For the twisted wire needles, you will need to punch a hole pattern in the leather first. Use a small finishing nail or leather awl. I anchor the buckskin by tacking it with thumb tacks to a small, thin square board 12" X 16" covered with fabric.

2. Most of you will be weaving from right to left. For those left handed people, like myself who have to take the time to transpose instructions, I show a left hand illustration. When you have your pattern completely graphed and colored and the warp threads attached, you are ready to begin weaving the beads into place. These instructions are for a strip ten beads wide.

For the right hand beader, begin with the first warp thread on the right. (reverse for the left) Assuming you have ten warps, you will need to string ten beads onto the first set of warp threads. This is the first, top row of your pattern. Push the beads up to the buckskin. Using a small crochet hook, split the weft threads and pull the warp threads back through the weft threads as illustrated in plates # 10 and # 11. Push each bead into place with your thumb.

The traditional way of pulling the warp threads through the weft threads is with your fingers. The crochet hook saves time and helps split the warps better. I also use a spring hair clip (illustrated, plate #12) to hold each finished row in place while stringing the next row of beads onto the next warp.

Always work each row with all the warp strands under that row. (illustrated in plate # 13) Remember that you are working on a downward slant and each row progresses one bead to the left as that row is finished.

3. String the second row of beads onto the next warp and push into place. Keep in mind that the pattern is being worked from right to left. So string the beads onto the warp thread in that order. The second row is placed exactly as the first and each following row.

4. Splitting the weave. You can split and reduce the width of the weave, doing one side of the split at a time. Begin at the right side using half the bead count. Weave half the row, leaving the other half of the warp threads hanging. Work on the right side of the split until that half is completed. If the unused half at the warps get in the way, tape across the **needles** and place them up out of the way. If you want to avoid getting the tape glue on the needles. Stick the needles through a piece of paper, then fold the paper across the needles and tape them up and out of the way. The crochet hook, hair clip, and taping needles to avoid tangling, can save an enormous amount of time in this technique.

5. When you are ready to bead the left side. Turn the strip over and tape the needles of the finished split side out of the way. By turning the strip over and beading the second split side, you have arranged the holes of the beads into a chevron pattern. If you are doing a continuation of a geometric pattern through each split side, don't turn your strip over unless you have designed your pattern for the chevron effect.

Each split has been illustrated in plates #14 and #15. You can split the tails of the strip as many times as the amount of beads used across the pattern will allow. I have never split smaller then a four bead count. However, I have seen a weave split to three and two bead count and it was a beautiful effect.

6. Bring the splits together into a full strip again by resuming the full pattern row. Allow all the warp needles to hang free. Make sure the split strips are exactly the same length in pattern row count. If you want the splits to hang into a drape around the neck increase the length of the outside split by two inches. Reduce the length of each split by 1/2" progressing to the inside split.

7. When you have completed the desired length of the weave, connect the warp thread to a piece of buckskin cut on the same slant as the weave. Use two chain embroidery stitches, pulling the chain tight to secure. Dab each knot with leather glue or clear nail polish. If you prefer to hide the knots with a coordinating bead, loop the warp needle through a bead and secure the thread to the knot under the bead.

My methods for constructing this technique is far from traditional, but the results are the same. We also show an alternative, **off loom weave** in this volume that resembles the side stitch. However, it only takes a single needle and thread.

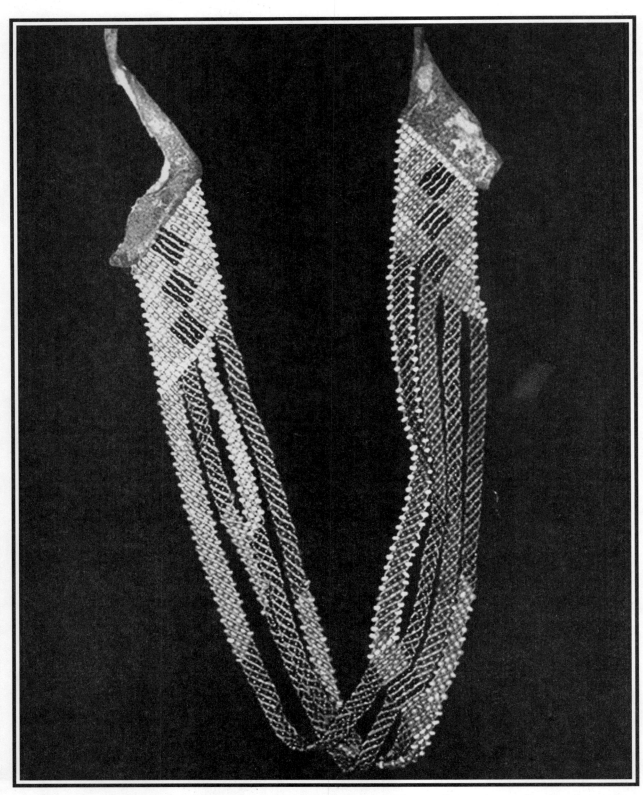

This lovely antique Ojibwa side stitched necklace done in soft shades of pink, green, yellow , lavender, purple and blue is part of the private collection of Custer Battlefield Trading Post, Crow Agency, Montana.

Side Stitch Weave

9 Plate

Attaching warp threads to leather, leaving knot in leather and needle hanging down.

8 Plate

Cut leather across on diagonal line

12 11 10 9 8 7 6 5 4 3 2 1

---Place first bead at this point, working right to left with slant of leather.

Regular beading needles can be used. However, there is less chance of tanglement and pricking the finger if you use the smallest twisted wire beading needles (size 12) designed for larger single strand beading. You must pre-punch the holes in leather for the twisted needle. A small finishing nail works well.

Warp threads should be approximately four times the lenghth of the beadwork.

String first pattern row of beads on # 1 warp. (Right to left on the pattern. Reverse for left hand beader.)

Side Stitich Continued

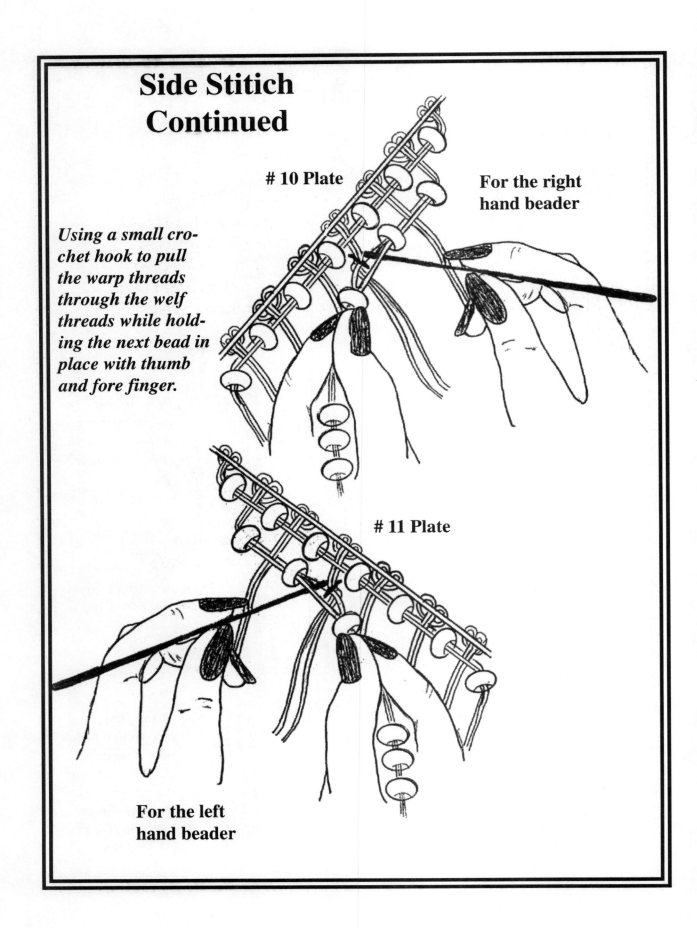

 # 10 Plate

For the right hand beader

Using a small crochet hook to pull the warp threads through the welf threads while holding the next bead in place with thumb and fore finger.

 # 11 Plate

For the left hand beader

Side Stitch Continued

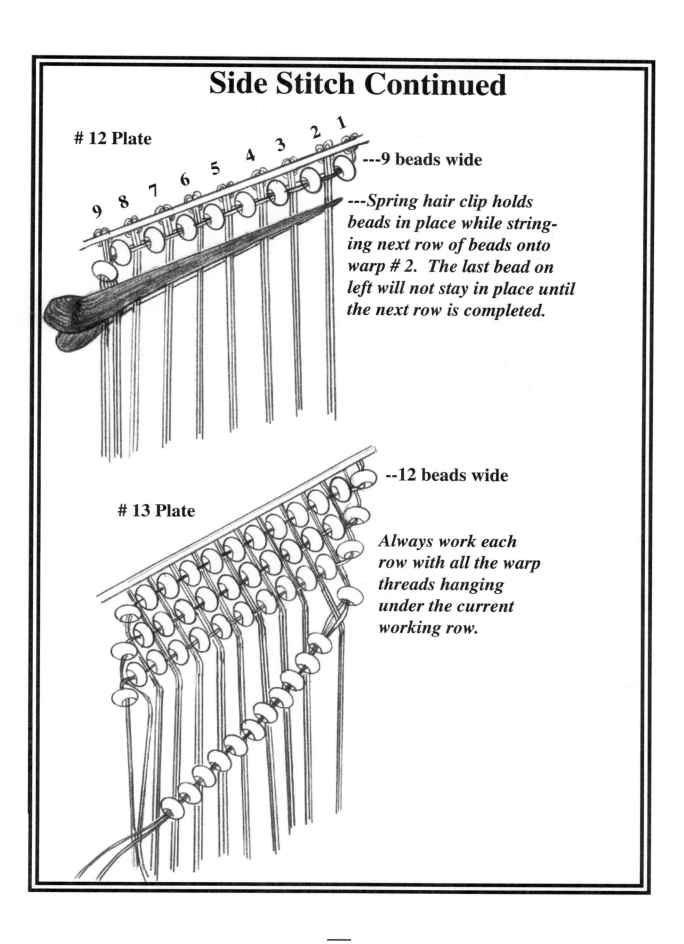

 # 12 Plate

9 8 7 6 5 4 3 2 1

---9 beads wide

---*Spring hair clip holds beads in place while stringing next row of beads onto warp # 2. The last bead on left will not stay in place until the next row is completed.*

--12 beads wide

 # 13 Plate

Always work each row with all the warp threads hanging under the current working row.

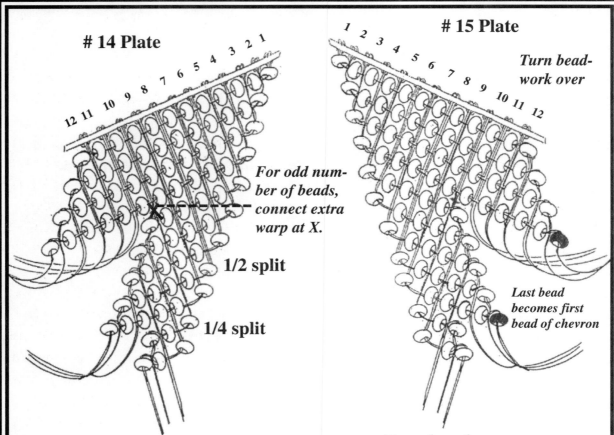

 # 14 Plate

12 11 10 9 8 7 6 5 4 3 2 1

For odd number of beads, connect extra warp at X.

1/2 split

1/4 split

 # 15 Plate

1 2 3 4 5 6 7 8 9 10 11 12

Turn bead-work over

Last bead becomes first bead of chevron

For original weave, complete the right side of each split, then the left side of small split. If you are using an odd number of beads across your pattern, you will need to connect an extra set of warp threads and needle to the finished beadwork (indicated with black X) in order to achieve an even amount of beads on each side of the split. The two center beads on each split row will stack slightly for the first three rows of the split.

For the chevron pattern, turn the beaded strip over after completing the right side. Begin with the outside warp of the small split. The first bead is already on the warp (indicated black bead). String remaining beads on warp and weave into place. Complete smallest split and tape the completed side out of the way, then complete the half split side.

38

Single Needle Side Stitch Weave

This technique is very similar in appearance to the traditional woven side stich, which used one needle to each set of warp threads. Both methods are a little more time consuming then other beading techniques, because you have to adjust your beading pattern for a diagonal direction. It also takes a little practice to adjust your mind to thinking diagonally, when it comes to designing a pattern for the side weave. All in all, the effort is well worth the finished product and it becomes easier each time you complete one. This is one of those projects where perseverance and self-discipline pays off.

If you have mastered "loom beading without a loom" (illustrated in Volume 3 of this series) this technique will be an extenuation of that method.

Step #1--This step begins with a seven bead looped circle. Two beads in the circle become the first two beads in row #1 (see plate #16). String remaining beads of row #1 and push them snugly against the circle.

Step #2--For the second row, pick up three beads (illustrated as beads #12, 13, and 14 in plate #17). Beads #11, 12, and 13 will be unattached until the next bead is stitched into place. To lock in bead #11 and #13. Follow the needle passage (arrows) illustrated in plate #18-A. Each row of the increase side of the weave begins the same as illustrated in plates #18 and #18-A. Each reducing row begins as illustrated in plates #19 and 19-A.

Splitting this weave into 1/2 and again into 1/4, entails the same increase and reducing stitches. To split the weave, begin reducing at the middle of the weave working form right to left. Reduce the first stitch and increase the left side, (see plate #33).

It's important that you finish each 1/2 and 1/4 splits before you weave the remaining half of the strip. It will keep you in prospective on the diagonal weave angle of your pattern while weaving the second 1/2 of the split.

If your pattern calls for an odd number of beads across the weave, you can still split the weave in the center by using the center bead twice as a pivot point for each side split (see plate #35).

For a chevron pattern, turn the weave over to complete the second half of the split.

For a challenging look to be admired by other beaders, turn the weave over and begin at the center pivot bead with a reducing stitch instead of an increase.

I'm sure you will agree that this technique was worth mastering and you'll use it again and again as enrichment to your beaded collection of jewelry.

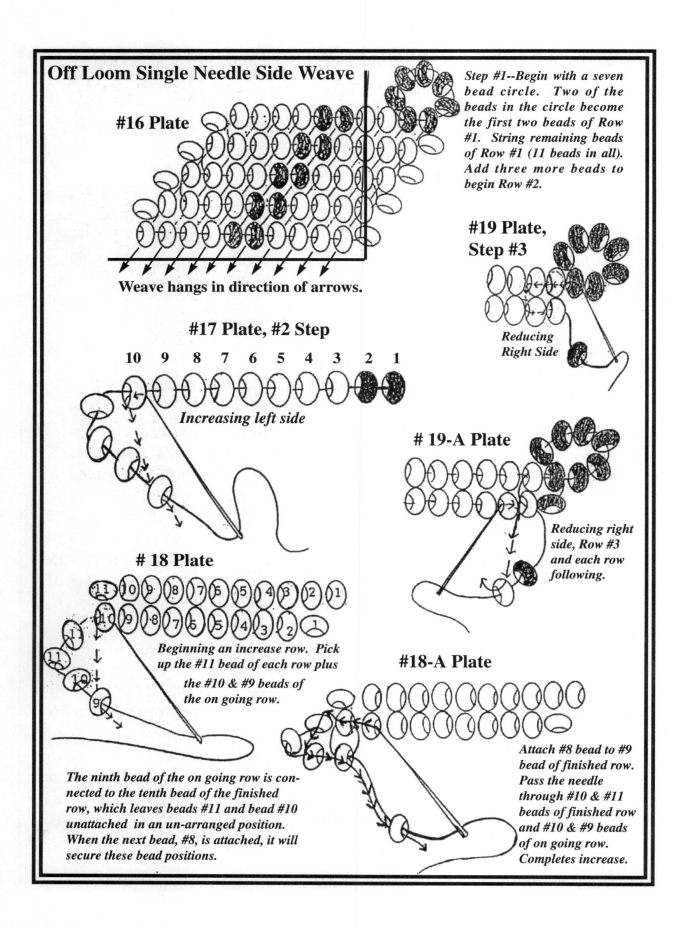

Off Loom Single Needle Side Weave

#16 Plate

Weave hangs in direction of arrows.

Step #1--Begin with a seven bead circle. Two of the beads in the circle become the first two beads of Row #1. String remaining beads of Row #1 (11 beads in all). Add three more beads to begin Row #2.

#19 Plate, Step #3

Reducing Right Side

#17 Plate, #2 Step

10 9 8 7 6 5 4 3 2 1

Increasing left side

 # 19-A Plate

Reducing right side, Row #3 and each row following.

18 Plate

11 10 9 8 7 6 5 4 3 2 1

11 10 9 8 7 6 5 4 3 2 1

Beginning an increase row. Pick up the #11 bead of each row plus the #10 & #9 beads of the on going row.

11

11

11

10

9

#18-A Plate

Attach #8 bead to #9 bead of finished row. Pass the needle through #10 & #11 beads of finished row and #10 & #9 beads of on going row. Completes increase.

The ninth bead of the on going row is connected to the tenth bead of the finished row, which leaves beads #11 and bead #10 unattached in an un-arranged position. When the next bead, #8, is attached, it will secure these bead positions.

Splitting Single Needle Side Stitch Weave

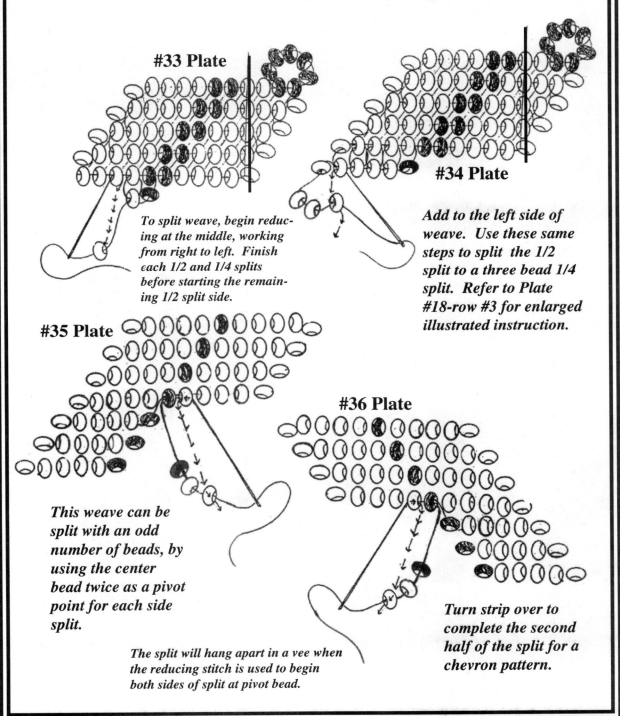

#33 Plate

To split weave, begin reducing at the middle, working from right to left. Finish each 1/2 and 1/4 splits before starting the remaining 1/2 split side.

#34 Plate

Add to the left side of weave. Use these same steps to split the 1/2 split to a three bead 1/4 split. Refer to Plate #18-row #3 for enlarged illustrated instruction.

#35 Plate

This weave can be split with an odd number of beads, by using the center bead twice as a pivot point for each side split.

The split will hang apart in a vee when the reducing stitch is used to begin both sides of split at pivot bead.

#36 Plate

Turn strip over to complete the second half of the split for a chevron pattern.

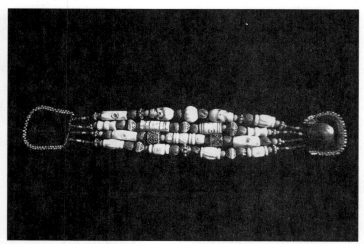

Frieda Bates has designed this beautiful bracelet with large , natural looking bone and ivory colored beads.

This medicine bag done by Frieda Bates is very bright and bold. The leather is turquoise with a rose colored closure. The fringe is also beaded in turquoise with compliments of black.

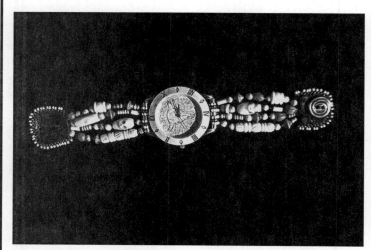

Frieda has created this very unique designed watch with earth-toned bone and ivory colored beads. The leather and button clasp adds enough finesse to this piece to give it a special flair.

Frieda's medicine bag was designed to compliment the watch on the left. The dark brown leather is combined with the natural tones of bone and ivory to finish the look.

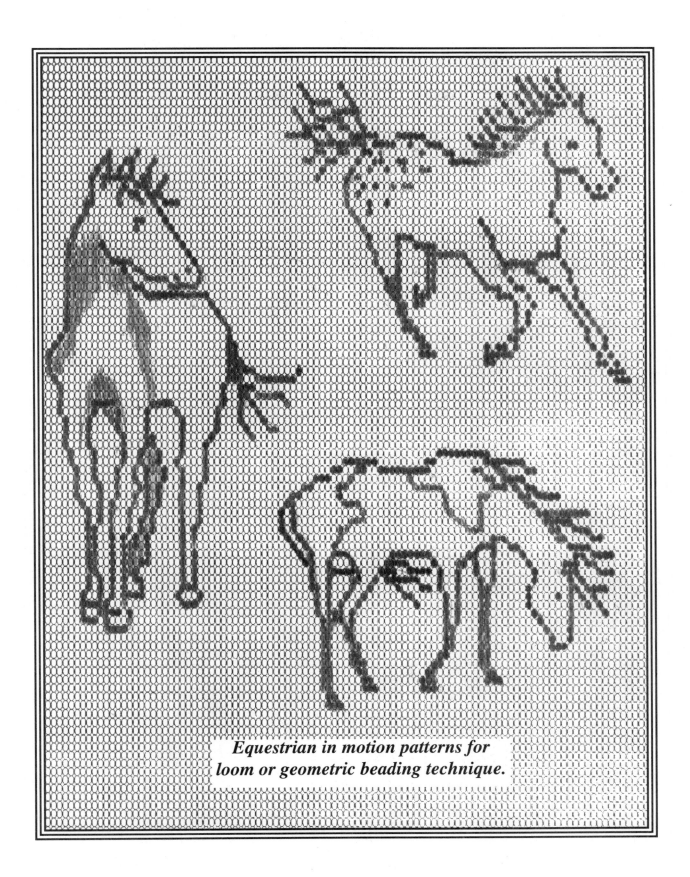

Equestrian in motion patterns for loom or geometric beading technique.

Southwestern
Applique

"African Beaded Pouch"

"Face Pouches On Trade Beads"

"Headdress of chiefton or high priest"

African Beadwork, Late 1800's

Amazingly, the Native African people created a beadwork very similar to the Native Americans. They are also known to do quill work. The trade beads of Africa are very popular in the United States and other parts of the world.

"Sun Face Medicine Pouch"

For research, I suggest, "The History of Beads" by Dubin. Photographs-- Authors Collection.

Beading on Garments

If you have ever looked for a special gift of "wearable art" that's affordable in boutiques, then you are ware of the dilemma a lot of shoppers face. You can create your own "secret source" of beautiful jewelry and decorative garments for the whole family. This series of books is designed to teach you techniques in beading and soft leather crafts while stimulating your own imagination and creative ability. There is no limit to the incredible variety of things you can do with beads. Once you start to bead, you begin to unlock your creative ability and soon discover the sensational ideas that have been locked up within yourself all the time. The "I love it" compliments will make you want to do more.

If you are fascinated with Native American regalia, you will enjoy the traditional techniques and patterns as well as contemporary and old world styles. You can create your own personal style from traditional to modern. You will enjoy the magic of beading made easy for you.

In this section, we illustrate some short cuts for beading on fabric garments. Showing the latest trends of that fashionable, fabulous, sparkling, dazzling look on jackets, dresses, coats, vests, shirts, sweaters, fleece sport shirts, ball caps, and t-shirts.

If you have glanced through any of the latest fashion catalogs, you must have noticed how beads have been used to enhance many vests and sweaters, while at the same time, making the price of that garment unaffordable to many people. Being in trendy style is very important to younger people. I am speaking from experience, since I have a 12 year old (who thinks she's going on 18) granddaughter that lives with me. Fashion has become one of her main subjects. So, what's a parent to do? Simple; cut the extravagant costs and create your own decorative wardrobe. Bead and trim the garments you are presently wearing.

To help you get more beading done in less time, I have illustrated in the following pages some shortcut, quick trick, time savers that can let you decorate garments in record time. Even if you have lots of time, you may want to use these techniques. You will get some impressive results.

Rather than do a separate piece of beadwork for each garment, begin by making a center piece that is detachable and can be transferred from garment to garment.

In this chapter, we show a photograph of a white buckskin flower being beaded and assembled. Very little beadwork is necessary, yet when finished, the complexity of each flower radiates a professional beaded look.

The pattern is simple. You don't have to use buckskin. Colored felt or heavy double bonded interfacing will work. Make a paper pattern for five sets of petals. Each petal set progresses in size and each flower takes five sets of petals. The two largest sets of petals are 2 1/2 inches across. The third is 2 inches across; the fourth, 1 1/2 inches and the last and center petal is one inch across. Each set has six petals. (see plate #26)

For the beadwork, do a simple edge stitch around each petal. (edge stitch is illustrated in plate #27)

When you have finished edging each set of petals, mark the center of each set and stack them, largest on the bottom, progressing to the smallest on the top center. Use a large bead of coordinating colors for the center. The large bead is held in place by using a seed bead for a turn bead. The needle and thread passes through the center of each set of petals from bottom to top and through the large bead. Put the turn bead on and pass the needle back through the large bead and petals. (see

plate #28) Tie and secure a knot with clear nail polish. Don't cut the needle loose yet. You will need to sew the pin back on (see plate #29). Turn each set of petals slightly, so that each smaller, top petal, laps over the gap in the larger bottom petals. You can sew or glue them into place with fabric glue. Next sew the pin back in place, on the center back of the flower.

Now that you have your center piece or pieces made, use seed beads of basic leaf colors and outline a leaf pattern directly on to garment. You can also edge stitch a green felt leaf on. Arrange the leaves so they will look good with or without the flower center piece.

The leaf does not necessarily have to be green. You can coordinate the bead colors to the color of the garment. Example: if your garment is turquoise, a green bead would clash, so use a gold or silver seed bead for the leaf outline.

There are so many options for decorating on garments. The techniques used for painting on fabric can be incorporated with beads. One of my favorites is cutting a flower or figure out a printed fabric. Gluing it onto a garment and edge stitch around it with beads and highlighting the center with beads.

For a quickie ornament, use thin craft wire designed for wire beading. String five or six inches of mixed colors of beads on to the wire. Fasten the wire to itself in one inch loops. Attach the loops to a pin back or earring wires and you have instant jewelry. Using wire as opposed to beading thread allows you to arrange the loops into flower petals or fan without connecting them to a backing. The wire holds the loops into place.

Beading with wire was a very popular technique during the first half of this century. Everything from buttons to belts was done with bead and wire. There are many lovely patterns that can be done using wire. However, we will try to cover that technique in another chapter.

The suggestions in this chapter are ideas that can be done using the techniques illustrated in this series.

For a great country western look, add a line of beaded fringe to the yoke seams of a shirt or blouse and attach a line beads around the cuff. You'll get stunning results. To add a finishing touch, use a beaded edge stitch or beaded whip stitch and bead around the brim of a western hat. An old hat looks great after beading. Or make a beaded hat band with buckskin streamers. A single beaded rosette pinned to the front of a western hat looks good also. Beaded button covers are quite popular and simple to make. Use any style earring; rosette, brickstitch, or wire beaded. Leave off the loop for the ear wire or ear post (see plate #31). Glue the earring onto the metal button cover cap (see plate #32) with epoxy glue, and

you have an interchangeable piece of jewelry added to your wardrobe. Leave the fringe on the earring; if you like the look of beaded fringe down the front of your garment.

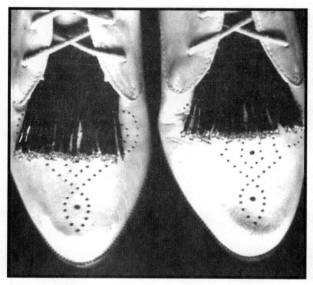

Lace up Roper boots are in style. The leather tabs on the Roper boot can be replaced with a beaded tap (see plate #30).

A nice touch for the ladies boots is adding a beaded ankle band with beaded fringes hanging all around.

For a Santa Fe look, attach a metal concho to the outside to the outside leg of a boot or jeans with buckskin lace. Add hand painted Peruvian beads to the end of the lace for trim. These conchos can be added to just about any garment. However, if you put them on a light weight fabric, use metal eyelets with interfacing behind them for holes in the fabric. Eyelets will keep the weight of the conchos from pulling through the fabric.

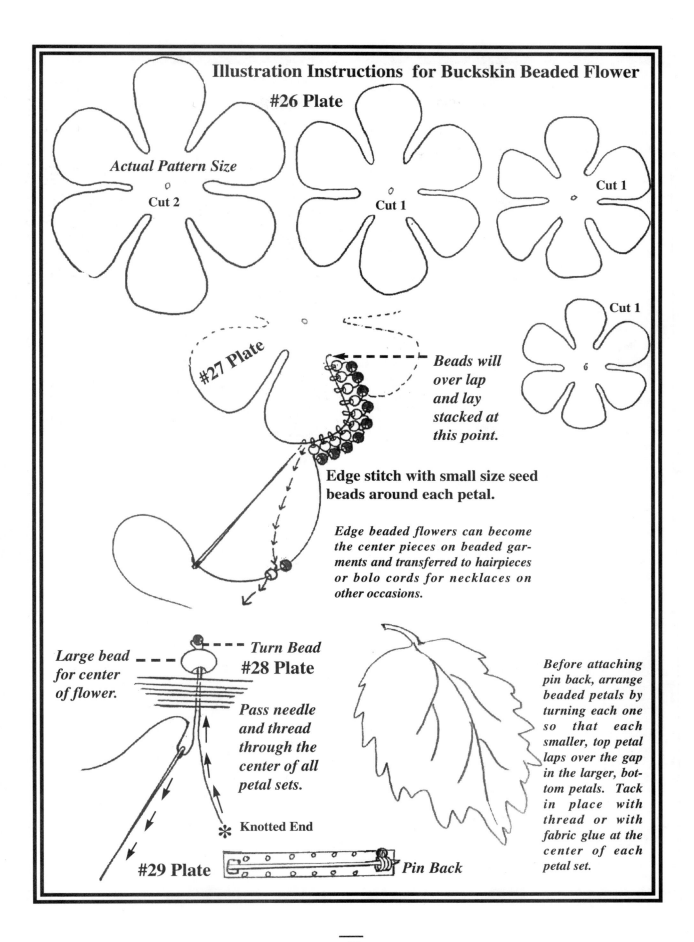

Illustration Instructions for Buckskin Beaded Flower

#26 Plate

Actual Pattern Size
Cut 2

Cut 1

Cut 1

Cut 1

#27 Plate

Beads will over lap and lay stacked at this point.

Edge stitch with small size seed beads around each petal.

Edge beaded flowers can become the center pieces on beaded garments and transferred to hairpieces or bolo cords for necklaces on other occasions.

Large bead for center of flower.

Turn Bead
#28 Plate

Pass needle and thread through the center of all petal sets.

✳ **Knotted End**

#29 Plate

Pin Back

Before attaching pin back, arrange beaded petals by turning each one so that each smaller, top petal laps over the gap in the larger, bottom petals. Tack in place with thread or with fabric glue at the center of each petal set.

Loom Beaded Boot Tabs

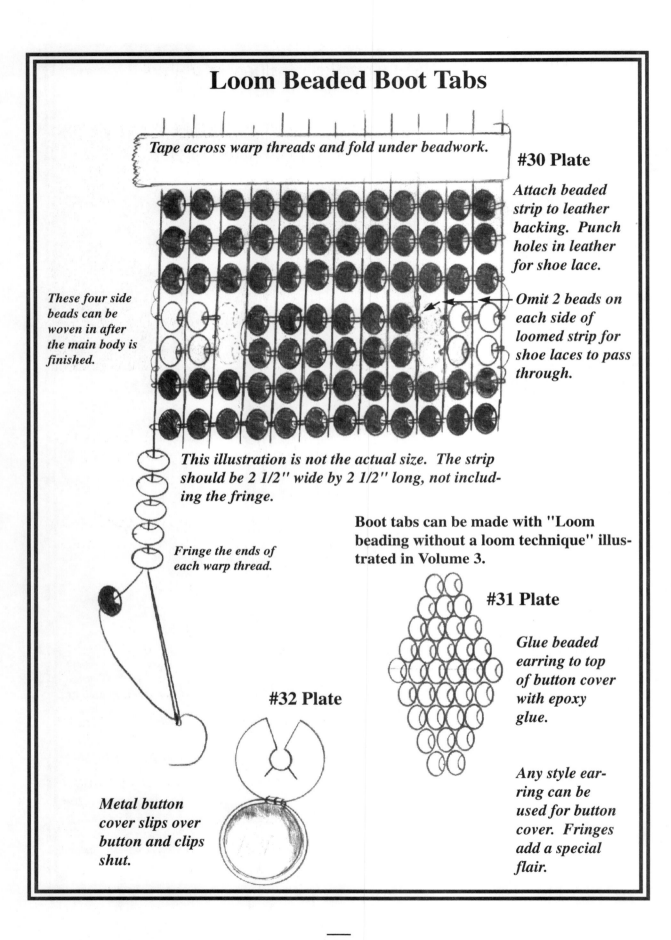

Tape across warp threads and fold under beadwork.

#30 Plate

Attach beaded strip to leather backing. Punch holes in leather for shoe lace.

These four side beads can be woven in after the main body is finished.

Omit 2 beads on each side of loomed strip for shoe laces to pass through.

This illustration is not the actual size. The strip should be 2 1/2" wide by 2 1/2" long, not including the fringe.

Fringe the ends of each warp thread.

Boot tabs can be made with "Loom beading without a loom technique" illustrated in Volume 3.

#31 Plate

Glue beaded earring to top of button cover with epoxy glue.

#32 Plate

Metal button cover slips over button and clips shut.

Any style earring can be used for button cover. Fringes add a special flair.

Garment Decor

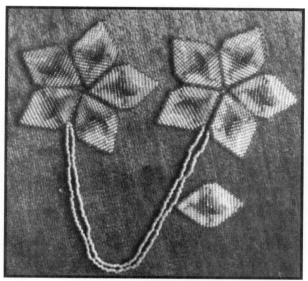

Flower petals arranged on garments. The same petal forms a leaf shape, which can be attached to a vine of beads.

Satin roses with green loops of 12/o cut beads for leaves on a sweater Pearl beads accent the roses.

For a unique and optional piece of beadwork that can be used as a hair piece, as a center piece for garment decor, attached to a purse, or worn on a bolo tie cord. (Picture in top left)

Shells in a leather fan.

This simple and quick "shells in a leather fan" technique will work for you. You will need three sea shell slices.

Step #1. Mix the seed beads with epoxy glue and fill holes in shells. Allow to dry completely.

Step #2. Arrange filled shell slices in a fan position.

Step #3. Cut leather piece in oval shape large enough to place shell fan on wrap bottom of the fan into leather oval. Glue into place and wrap and tie leather lace around bottom of fan. Do an edge stitch around the outside of the leather fan. Secure the sea shells by sewing through the bottom opening of shells and through the leather. Add larger beads to the end of leather lace or edge stitch around the ends of the lace to match the fan.

"Blue Eagle Feather" pouches with metal cones, accompanied by a geometrice pattern pouch. Courtesy of Custer Battlefield Trading Post, Crow Agency, Montana.

"Crow Design" pouches in vibrant blues, yellow, and reds. On display at Custer Battlefield Trading Post.

These pouches which are also on display at Custer Battlefield Trading Post, the beadwork is done is various colors and designs as well as different sizes and shapes. Plains Indians.

Antique Pouch. The body of this pouch is beaded primarily in red, white and blue, but fringed in red, green, white, blue, and yellow. Very well preserved.

Rosette style beaded moccasins in blue, red, white, yellow, and black. Courtesy of Custer Battlefield Trading Post, Crow Agency, Montana.

These red, white, blue, and black beaded moccasins are fully beaded for ceremonial dress. On display at Custer Battlefield Trading Post.

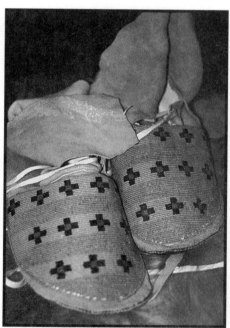

The beadwork on these Northern Plains moccassins is done is turquoise, pink, and a navy blue. Custer Battlefield Trading Post.

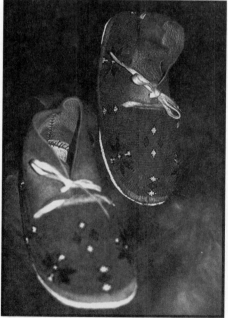

In this photograph are Northern Plains beaded moccasins in blue, red, and white. Courtesy of Custer Battlefield Trading Post, Crow Agency, Montana.

Tommie Prentice has created this beautiful porcelain indian doll. She has implemented the buckskin dress and the beadwork to create this adorable little indian girl.

These porcelain indian dolls are not only adorable, but excellent craftsmanship. Leather work and beadwork have been incorporated into both projects to create that traditional look. These photographs are courtesy of Creative Corner, Miami, Oklahoma. Beautiful!

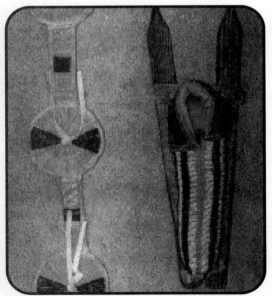

Antique quill blanket strip on left in gold and purple and doll cradleboard on the right beaded in green yellow, white and red. Courtesy of Custer Battlefield Trading Post.

Antique beaded blanket. The royal blue background is accented with beautiful pink flowers around the entire outer edge. Courtesy of Custer Battlefield Trading Post, Crow Agency, Montana.

Snake effigy, used in healing the sick. Courtesy of The Hastings Museum, Hastings, Nebraska.

This buffalo horn is on display at The Hastings Museum. Quill work has been incorporated with the horn to enhance the look.

Beaded leggings from the Plains Indians in red, white, and blue. Courtesy of The Hastings Museum, Hastings, Nebraska.

Beaded blanket strip (Northern Plains). This piece has been beaded red, blue, lavender, black and ecru. The Hastings Museum.

This white, green, red, yellow and black riffle scabbard was made in the late 1800's.

Beaded pipe bag with quill fringe in red, white, blue, and green. The Hastings Museum, Hastings, Nebraska.

This lovely pouch is beaded with a white background and accented by red, black, turquoise and yellow. Sioux Trading Post, Rapid Ctiy, South Dakota.

Miniature pipe and bag, Sioux (left) and miniature carrier and doll (right) Hastings Museum, Hastings, Nebraska.

Beaded pouch. The Hastings Museum, Hastings, Nebraska.

Ute style cradle made by Dawna Jolliff of Henderson, Nevada.

Close-up of Ute style cradle by Dawna Jolliff. See page 65 for description information.

Northern Pauite cradle from Pyramid Lake, Nevada. Maker unknown. Photographs are from a Private Collection. See page 65 for details.

Northern Paiute/Shoshone cradle from Walker Lake, Nevada. Maker: Emma Copeland. See page 65 for details.

Kootenai cradle from western Montana. Maker unknown. Private Collection. See page 65 for information.

Warm Springs cradle from Warm Springs, Oregon. Maker unknown. Private Collection. See page 65 for details.

Shoshone cradle, 1915 from West Yellowstone, Montana. Maker, Mary Wagon. Private Collection. See page 65 for information.

Close-up of beadwork on Shoshone cradle. Private Collection.

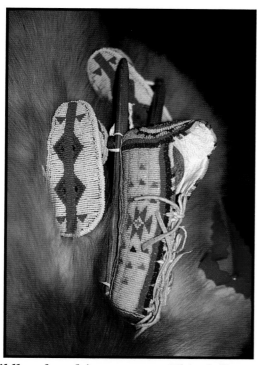

Childhood and innocence. This doll cradle and with matching child's moccasins brings back memories of our youth. Photograph courtesy of Custer Battlefield Trading Post, Crow Agency, Montana.

This beautifully beaded full size cradleboard is originated from the Plains Indian style. Traditional colors are used in this design. Photograph courtesy of Custer Battlefield Trading Post, Crow Agency, Montana.

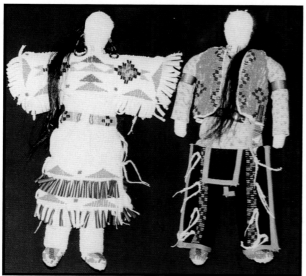

Beaded Dolls. Female--metal cones for jingle. The lazy stitch beadwork is used with buffalo hair for the scalp. Male--sports a handmade miniature knife with scabbard and concho belt. Brass arm and beaded vest. Authors collection.

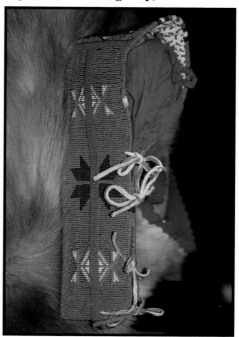

Beaded Doll Cradle. Bold red, turquoise, yellow, and blue. Adorable! Photograph courtesy of Custer Battlefield Trading Post, Crow Agency, Montana.

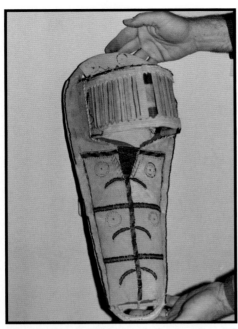

Apache doll cradleboard from the 1860's. "Putt" at Custer Battlefield Trading Post, Crow Agency, Montana holds this prize artifact from his private collection.

This elegantly beaded and well preserved cradle was done by "Happi Little Calf". 1880's wife of "Old Crow" Southern Cheyenne. Private collection of "Put & Jill" at Custer Battlefield Trading Post, Crow Agency, Montana.

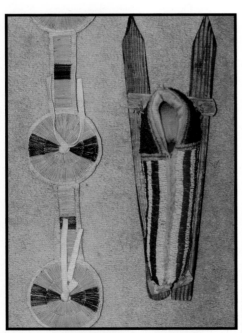

Comanche doll cradle made in 1890 and quill rosette blanket strip. Photograph courtesy of Custer Battlefield Trading Post, Crow Agency, Montana.

These two beautifully beaded Crow Indian cradleboards are on display at Custer Battlefield Trading Post, Crow Agency, Montana.

Beaded buckskin shirt and belt. The vast amount of fringe combined with the simplicity of the beadwork is very striking. Photograph courtesy of Custer Battlefield Trading Post, Crow Agency, Montana.

Fully beaded pouch. This is the depiction of the indian war chief on his majestic horse. The piece is done in lazy stitch. Courtesy of Custer Battlefield Trading Post, Crow Agency, Montana.

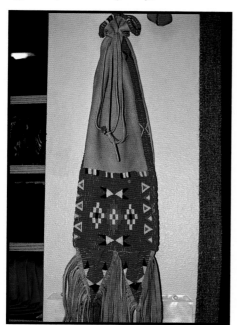

The medicine pouch or pipe bag of the Plains Indian design is done in blue, white, red and black and is on display at Custer Battlefield Trading Post, Crow Agency, Montana.

This lovely antique beaded pouch is in need of a little repair, but still reflects the elegantly, elaborate pattern and detail of the 1800's. Photograph courtesy of Custer Battlefield Trading Post, Crow Agency, Montana.

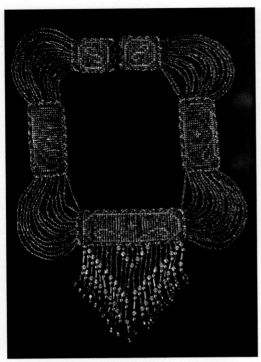

Jude Biegert of Bead Lady Designs has created this elegant necklace in ecru, golds and bronze with accents of black. Notice the majestic eagle head.

Jude Biegert has created this necklace, which she entitles "First Love: Bermuda Blue" This multi-colored design has almost a victorian look. Very elegant!!

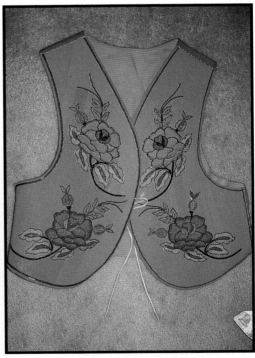

This brain-tanned shirt has been complimented by red and orange-gold roses. Pants have been made to match (not shown). Photograph courtesy of Custer Battlefield Trading Post, Crow Agency, Montana.

What an exquisite beaded vest! The blue vest with pink lining is accentuated by the beautiful roses done in pink and blue with darker coloring for shading. Photograph courtesy of Custer Battlefield Trading Post, Crow Agency, Montana.

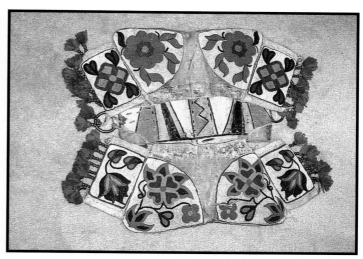

Exquisite beaded antique saddle. Photograph is courtesy of Custer Battlefield Trading Post.

This beautiful fully beaded pouch is done in vibrant reds, greens, browns and blues. Photograph courtesy of Custer Battlefield Trading Post, Crow Agency, Montana.

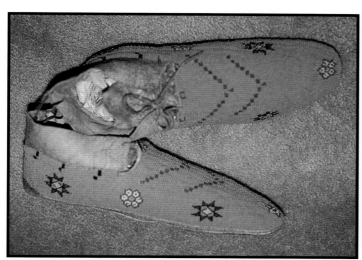

This photograph of beaded moccassins is courtesy of Custer Battlefield Trading Post, Crow Agency, Montana. The beadwork has a blue background with accents of red, yellow, green, and black. Made in the 1800's.

Beaded moccasins from the 1800's. Notice the majestic, beaded bird in blue, yellow, green, and red and the surrounding flowers in alternate colors. Courtesy of Custer Battlefield Trading Post.

Melody Abbott has out done herself again! This beautiful loom beaded strip for a cradleboard has been done in fabulous, vibrant colors.

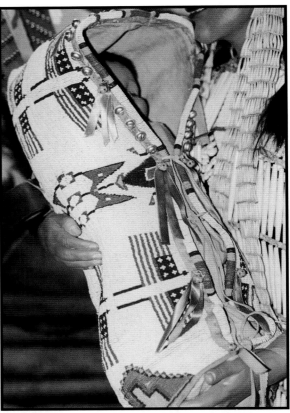

Northern Plains beaded cradleboard. Notice the red, white and blue flags. Miniture brass buttons encompass the cradleboard hood. Photograph courtesy of The Hastings Museum, Hastings, Nebraska.

Beaded buckskin dress. Background done in Cheyenne pink with red, white and blue geometric design. Plains Indians, late 1800's.

This adorable beaded buckskin child's dress and dolls were made in the late 1800's in red, blue, white, yellow and black.

Descriptive Information Of Cradleboards And Beadwork Shown In The Color Pages

On page 57 and 58 of the color section, we begin to show the beauty and direct purpose for each cradleboard and the significance of the design. On page 57, top left, Dawna Jolliff displays the Ute cradle that she has made herself. The yellow leather covering indicates this is for a girl baby. White leather is used for boys cradles. The protective hood is made from reed (natural and dyed) and the back is made from wood. The beadwork in this photograph was done on a loom.

The top right photograph is simply a close-up to show the exquisite and intricate detail of beadwork. Dawna has done a marvelous job!

The Northern Paiute cradle from Pyramid Lake, Nevada is from a private collection. The bottom left photograph shows that the frame is made from bent chokecherry branches, covered with a woven willow mat. The hood is also woven of willow and design indicates that this is a girls cradle (zig-zags or diamonds). It is covered in brain-tanned and smoked buckskin. Each bead in the design is sewn on individually. (Typical of Northern Paiute and Shoshone work)

The bottom right on page 57 is from the Northern Paiute/Shoshone cradle from Walker Lake, Nevada made by Emma Copeland. The frame is constructed of bent chokecherry branches, covered with a woven willow mat. The hood is also woven of willow and design indicates that this was for a boy baby (diagonal lines). It is covered in commercially tanned buckskin and floral beadwork is done by the applique method. This piece is also from a private collection.

In the color section on page 58, the top left cradleboard is a Kootenai cradle from western Montana. The designer in this case is unknown. The back is made from wood covered in brain-tanned and smoked buckskin. A leather "bib" covers the lacing. The beadwork is done by the applique method.

In the upper right corner on page 58, we see Warm Springs cradle from Warm Springs, Oregon. Again, the creator is unknown. The back is made of wood covered with commercially tanned buckskin. The hood is made of a bent branch also leather covered. The beadwork on the body is a combination of lazy stitch and individual bead sewing. The hood has wrapped beadwork with cowrie shell and tile bead dangles, for the child's amusement.

The Shoshone cradle of page 58, bottom left, is 1915 from West

Yellowstone, Montana. The artist of this cradleboard is Mary Wagon. Here again, the back is wood covered with brain-tanned buckskin. The carrying strap is made from and older sinew-sewn beaded belt with brass tacks. Each bead in floral design is individually sewn. The border is the lazy stitch.

A close-up of Mary Wagon's beadwork is shown on the Shoshone cradle in the bottom right photograph.

Custer Battlefield Trading Post displays an exquisite cradleboard, pictured on page 59, top right. This fully beaded split frame board is meticulous in the placing of each bead. The four large eagle feathers beaded into the geometric design are exact on both sides of the board. A lot of planning and care has gone into constructing this beauty.

In the top left photograph on page 59, a doll cradleboard is shown with a pair of infant, beaded moccasins. Notice how the cradle resembles a larger moccasin in shape. The lower right photograph is a larger doll cradle. Both are beautifully beaded. Courtesy of Custer Battlefield Trading Post.

The floral beaded cradle cover shown on page 60, top right, is one of the masterpieces of a by-gone generation. The photograph does not do justice to this lovely piece. The beading techniques used are lane stitch for background and applique for floral. Notice how even the lanes are beaded. The lane line around the floral are dis-tinctively exact. The creator "Happy Little Calf" shows her lover for baby and beading.

On page 64, top right, we show a fully beaded cradleboard of the Northern Plains Indian of the late 1800's. This patriotically beaded cover shows how devoted the Native American people are to the flag of the United States of America. Courtesy of The Hastings Museum, Hastings, Nebraska.

It is customary to dress in your most outstanding garments for a wedding. The Native American traditionally dresses the bride in an elaborately beaded, fringed, white, brain-tanned leather dress. The groom is just as stunning wearing a beaded wedding vest such as the one pictured on page 62 (lower right). Courtesy of Battlefield Trading Post.

Unlike modern wedding attire, used once and put away. These beaded garments are used for special ceremonies and pow wows throughout the life of the bride and groom. When the garment wears out, the beads are cut away and saved for another project. That is why beadwork that is still in tack from the past centuries are such a prized possession. Each time the beads were recycled and new beads added, it became harder to date the garment. The production of seed beads vary a great deal over two centuries. The antique, hand crafted quality of some beads very distinctive.

Alternate Transition From Cradleboard to Backpack

Last year I contracted Melody Abbott to loom a large strip of beadwork for a cradleboard I planned to construct. I gave her the dimensions needed for the project and she created a gorgeous, in depth beaded strip that takes your breath away to gaze upon it. The strip is large enough to cover both sides and top of a cradleboard, however, I had an ulterior motive in mind.

Cradleboards are lovely to look at, but have no optional use other than exactly what they are made for. Not wanting to hang this beautiful piece of beadwork on my wall attached to a cradleboard, where few people would have a chance to admire it. I converted the beaded cradleboard to a beaded backpack that can be used and admired frequently. It really adds a look of beaded elegance to my wardrobe and I'm quick for an excuse to use it.

Melody Abbott has a natural talent for beading and expresses her ability to transfer her creative patterns to the loom in a wonderful artistic way. You can not help, but recognize the individuality of her artistry. She has plans of publishing her patterns in the future.

In the color section, there is a full view of this beaded strip.

Choosing The Right Materials

One of the most frequently asked questions is "how do you choose the right materials for basic beading?"

First, decide which technique you will use and begin by checking off the materials needed beginning with the foundation. For example; if you prefer applique beading, you will need a strong fabric or soft beading leather to attach the beads. Next is an embroidery hoop for holding the fabric. Decide on a pattern and you will need a complete set of colors in felt tip pens. Photocopy any of the specially sketched drawings and color them in with the felt tip pens or color pencils. Pre-programming your color pattern saves time and lets you have a glimpse at what your finished piece will look like before you put a lot of time and materials into a project. Harmonious colors come from the eye of the beader, (when able to make changes before hand). Imaginative color ideas need to be written down or colored in before they are forgotten.

Now that you have the foundation materials together, you will need needles to fit the size of your beads. An appropriate sized beading thread and shallow containers to keep your bead colors separated, plus a good light to see by, an easy chair and television tray.

Throughout this series, we have exposed special techniques that show how to enhance a plain pattern with a combination of fringing and edging to make a dazzling eye catcher. Each volume contains projects never before revealed. You will find time saving short cut techniques explained.

Getting back to basic materials, you will need a fabric glue to glue the paper pattern to the beading leather or fabric, a small thread scissors, and a pair of needle flat nose pliers. Now all you will need is a little time to get started. This fascinating craft will entertain you as well as enhance your wardrobe.

As you work your way through this series of books, you will find dozens of beading techniques and hundreds of patterns and suggestions for your project. Each color sections will inspire you, for they show enchanting beadwork of beaders from different areas of the United States and Canada.

I encourage you to become involved with this incredibly inspirational, rewarding craft. You will be amazed how easy it is to learn and how much pleasure you will have in being able to say "I have mastered this time honored craft". Your friends will love the gifts you make and you will enjoy their admiration.

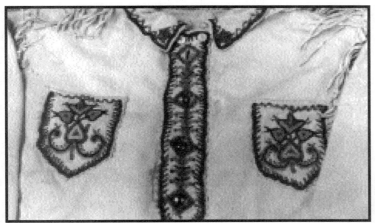

Beaded white buckskin shirt. The collar, pockets and lapel of this shirt are detailed in blue, red, yellow, green, and lavender. The Hastings Museum, Hastings, Nebraska.

This beaded infants hood has a white background with accents of lavender, purple, blue, and green. Photograph courtesy of The Hastings Museum, Hastings, Nebraska.

This display shows dentalium shell hair ties with bone hair pipe beaded front cover. The shoulder line has been beaded with glass seed beads. Cowie shells ornate the sleeves and across the front and back below the beadwork. The belt has been made with silver conchos. Courtesy of The Hastings Museum.

Author's collection. Hair piece rosettes with peyote stitch on feathers. Beaded in exciting, bright colors of blue, red, yellow, black and white in 13/o cut.

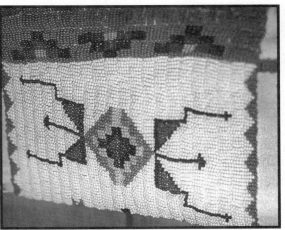

This buckskin beaded pouch is done in vibrant blues, red, yellow, black on a white background. Courtesy of Custer Battlefield Trading Post, Crow Agency, Montana.

*Southwestern
for Rosette
Applique*

Lois McCoy of Tandy Leather, Redding, California has made this white beaded buffalo with shading of grey and black. Very majestic!

Jennifer Tallbear made these dream catchers. The one on the left is pink with purple accents and the right, turquoise with white. She has used silver, stone and glass beads in this project.

Leather pouch was made by using the lane stitch with circled beads on fringe. Photograph courtesy of Sioux Trading Post, Rapid City, South Dakota.

This beautiful beaded knife scabbard is on display at Custer Battlefield Trading Post. The top is done in yellow and green and the bottom, in mauve, green and white.

Woodland style applique beadwork on fringed collar. Displayed at The Hastings Museum, Hastings, Nebraska.

Sioux buckskin dress with beaded yoke, done in red and blue beads and Cowie shell fringe. The Hastings Museum.

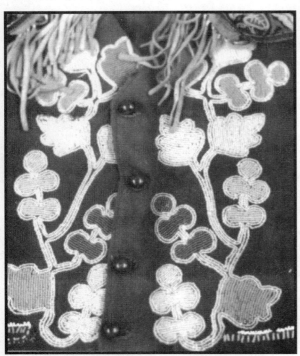

Osage appliqued shirt with pastel colors of light pink, raspberry, yellow, blue, and green. The Hastings Museum.

Sioux buckskin shirt (1860). Decorated with quill worked strips on the breast, sleeves, and across the shoulders.

Using color for dimension. Stacked blocks with a diagonal point radiates an illusion of depth.

Stacked inner woven diamonds in alternate colors give depth to this graph.

Applique or overlay patterns

The Carousel Horse

For a unique and different look, hang short fringes around the saddle and the ribbon streamers on the pole, mane, and tail

Carousel colors are taken from antique design.

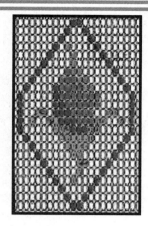

Color Pattern for Front Cover of Volume Seven

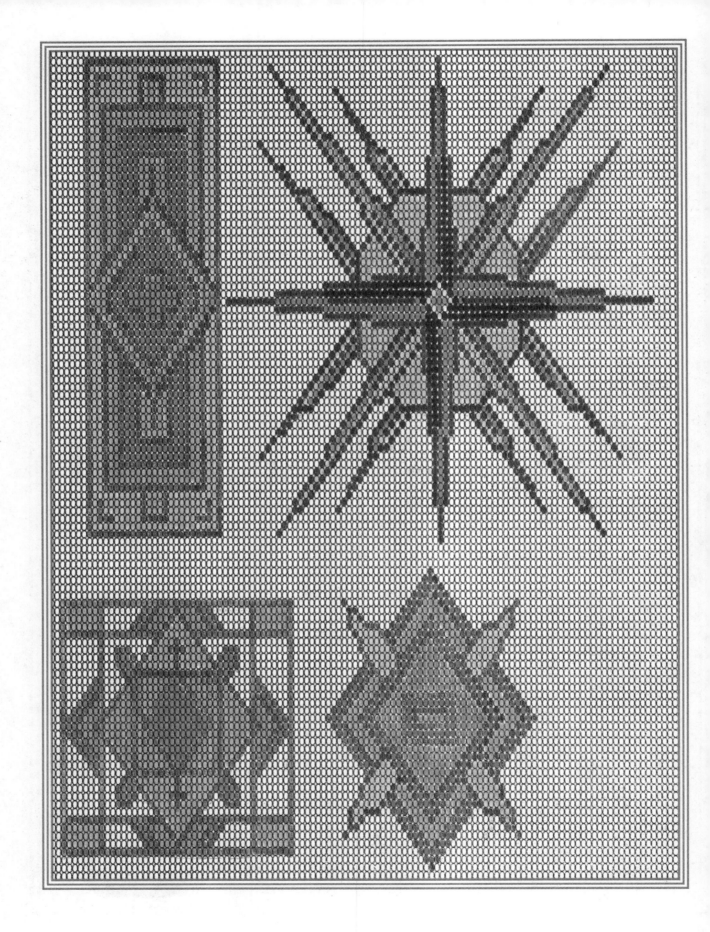

Pattern Designs

1. Menominee
2. Menominee
3. Chippewa

Geometric patterns for loom or off loom techniques.

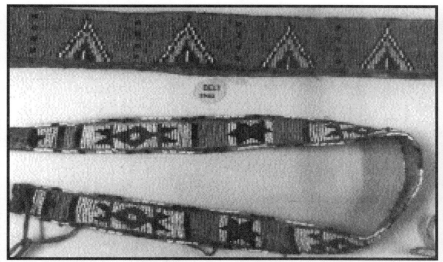

Belt and hat band. The belt at the top has been beaded in blue with accents of red, yellow, and white. This set is on display at The Hastings Museum, Hastings, Nebraska.

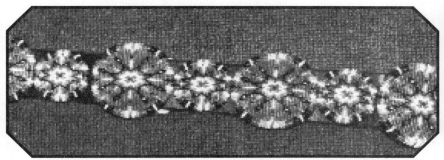

Beaded rosette concho belt in beautiful, vibrant colors of turquoise, pink, black, white, and yellow. Photograph is courtesy of Custer Battlefield, Crow Agency, Montana.

This handsome beaded hat band was originated from the Winnebago Indians. Courtesy of The Hastings Museum, Hastings, Nebraska.

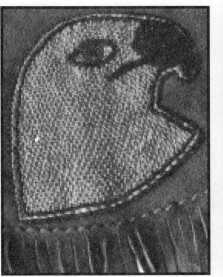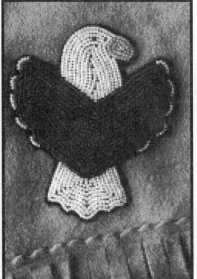

The bottom two photographs to the left are of Canadian beadwork done with applique on a buckskin vest. These majestic birds are shown in white, brown, and yellow-gold. The eagle head on the left is appliqued to the back of the vest and the eagle in flight has been attached to the front lapel. The photograph is courtesy of Jennifer Tallbear.

Eastern Woodland Prehistoric Art Designs
Engraved on pottery of the Gulf Coast group from Alabama to Florida.

Kachina
Applique

Southwestern for Applique

Beaded bandolier bag from the middle 1800's. Top is loomed strip. Bottom has eleven loomed tasseled strips added to the square loomed pouch.

Beaded bandolier bag from the middle 1800's. Done in various shades of green complemented with red, black, yellow and white.

This beautiful beaded bandolier bag from the 1800's has been appliqued in yellow, green, black, red, and blue.

Beaded pouch. The top is beaded and bottom half is dyed quill work. Courtesy of Sioux Trading Post, Rapid City, South Dakota.

Beaded pouches and arm bands. Photograph courtesy of The Hastings Museum, Hastings, Nebraska.

The beaded bags on this page, cover the last one hundred years of some beading styles used by the Native American.

The Last of the Herd
(For applique or overlay technique)

Doris Barnes spends a lot of time beading colorful earrings for her beading business. These lovely designs are part of her personal collection.

My sister-in-law, Doris Barnes has designed and beaded a variety of Christmas earrings. It's time now to give Christmas, 1994 some thought for beaded gifts.

Toni Earrie has designed an authentic looking drum earring made with goat skin. Great idea! The chili peppers are a hot item, also.

African beaded bracelet. Made at the turn of this century. Authors collection.

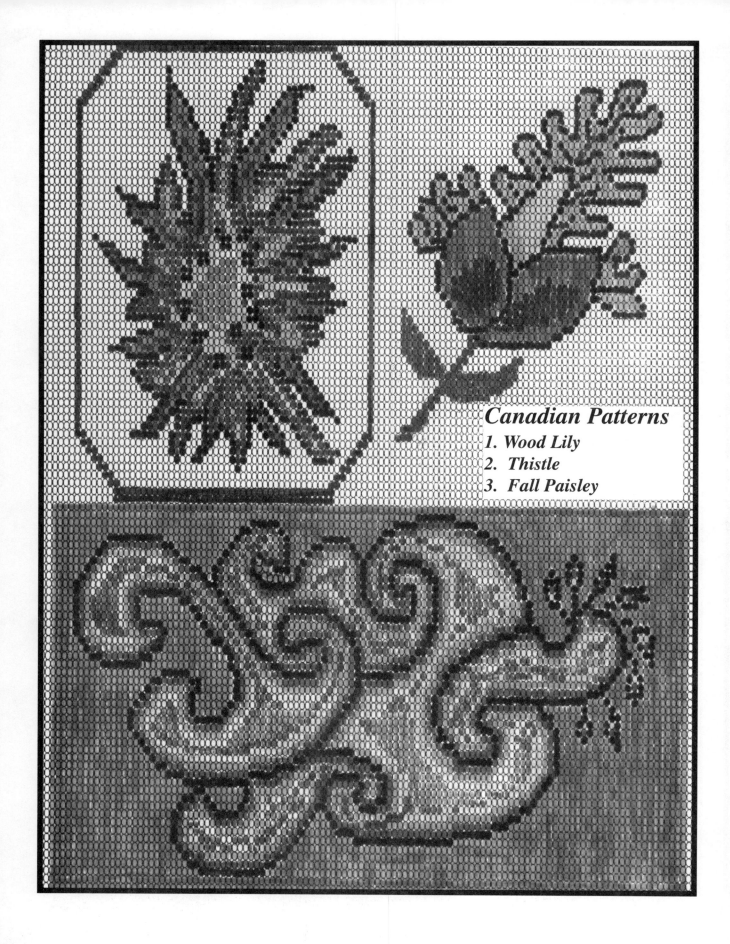

Canadian Patterns
1. Wood Lily
2. Thistle
3. Fall Paisley

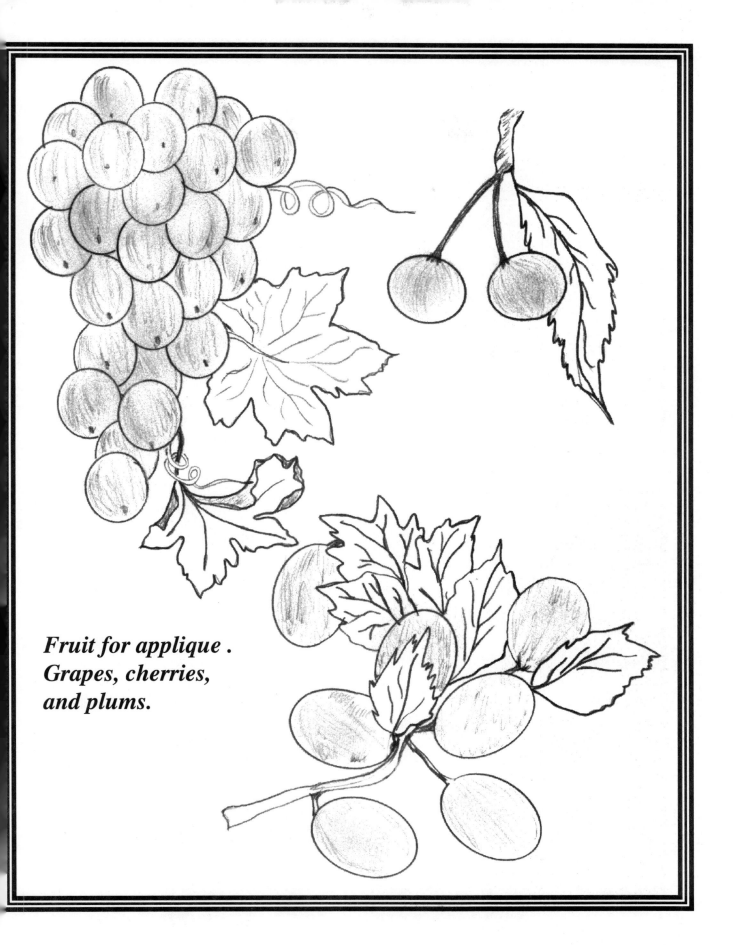

*Fruit for applique .
Grapes, cherries,
and plums.*

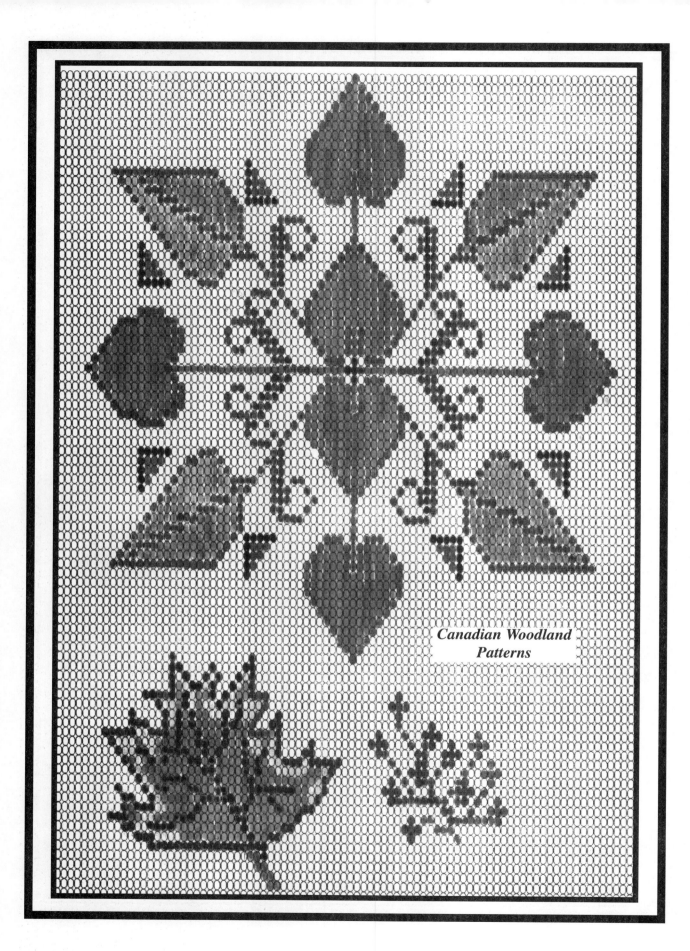

Canadian Woodland
Patterns

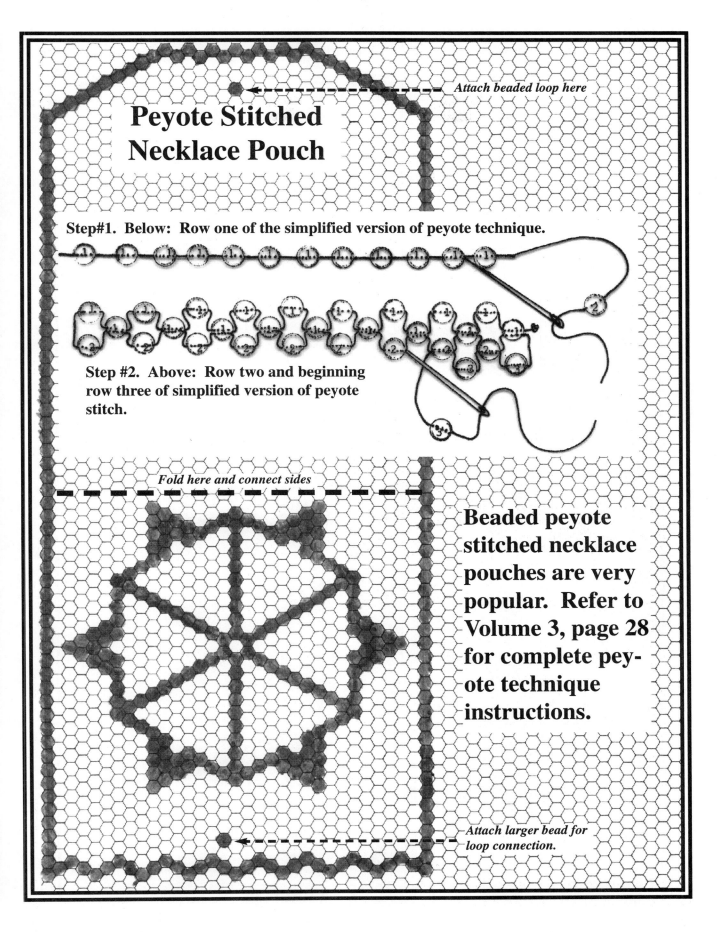

Attach beaded loop here

Peyote Stitched Necklace Pouch

Step#1. Below: Row one of the simplified version of peyote technique.

Step #2. Above: Row two and beginning row three of simplified version of peyote stitch.

Fold here and connect sides

Beaded peyote stitched necklace pouches are very popular. Refer to Volume 3, page 28 for complete peyote technique instructions.

Attach larger bead for loop connection.

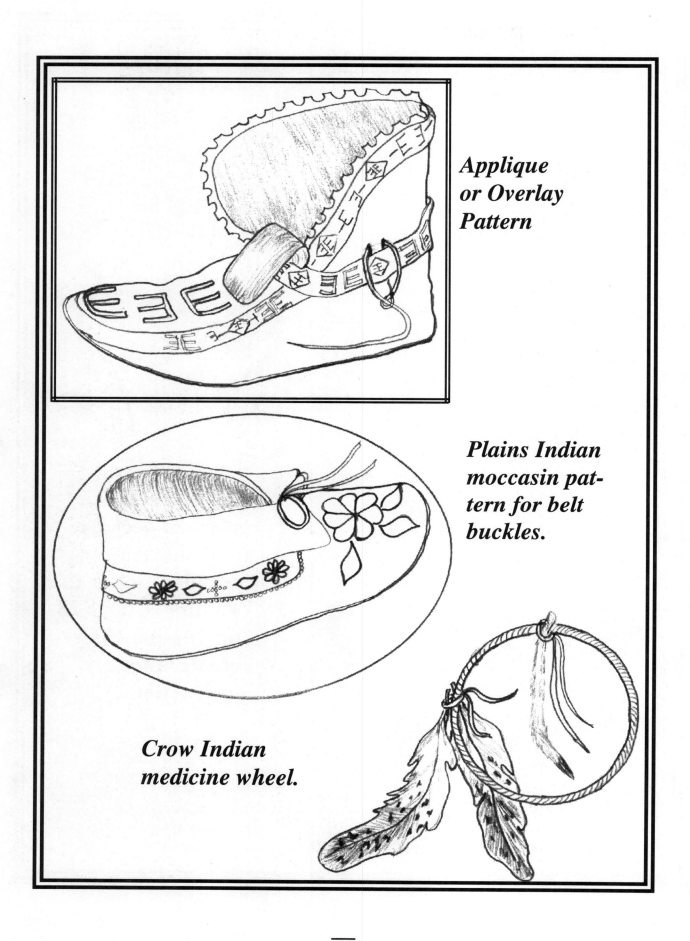

Applique or Overlay Pattern

Plains Indian moccasin pattern for belt buckles.

Crow Indian medicine wheel.

Front Cover Beadwork in Progress

The front cover of this volume was created by the author using some of the time saving short cuts talked about throughout this series.

The Navajo loomer is photocopied from a water color done in 1951 (artist unknown). However, the copy was enlarged and altered slightly for bead-work, then printed on light weight interfacing that was edge glued to a sheet of regular copy paper; allowed to dry, then hand-fed through the copy machine. (Described in Volume Six, pages seven and eight, "A Time Saving Secret".)

The interfacing is gently separated from the sheet of copy paper then glued onto the beading leather with fabric glue. Next, I colored in some of the areas with pastel felt tip pens.

Notice the background of loom warp strings have been darkened and will show through the eggshell color beads when finished. The bottom area of the loom has one-third of a geometric rug finished and will be beaded with the lane (lazy) stitch. Size 14/o Japanese beads are being used. The beaded area is 13 1/2" in height by 11 1/2" in width. There is about 17 hours of beading time involved at this point. Total hours; 65 hours to completion.

Related Volumes Of The Beads to Buckskins Series

Volumes are available directly from the publishers or through your bookstore or craft center. Each volume will always be available.

Beads to Buckskins Publications

P. O. Box 296

Hill City, Kansas 67642

(913) 674-2333

Volume One: If you are a beginner, you can learn "Native American Indian techniques" the easy way with over 180 easy to follow patterns both graphed and freehand. Also included; loom beading, the peyote stitch, overlay and applique stitch, the lane or (lazy) stitch, five edge or fret stitching techniques, loom beading without a loom, the brick stitch, daisy chain, geometric designs and patterns, plus a beautiful color section.

Volume Two: Has over 200 patterns including a moccasin and buckskin shirt pattern with unusual looming techniques. Included in this volume; split loomed necklace instructions, secrets revealed in beading, spanish lace earrings, silhouettes, cradleboard earring, chevron chain, indian flower, peyote stitch overlay or applique stitch. Eight pages of full color photograph section.

Volume Three: Shows some prize winning beadwork in the color section, as well as instructions and patterns of how to do it. The loom beading without a loom technique has been illustrated to show how to complete a split loom necklace without the use of a loom. Another feature in Volume Three, is how to bead with stone cabochons incorporated with seed beads to make a beautiful and unusual piece of jewelry. You will learn how to make a squaw dress with moccasin pattern instructions, brain tanning techniques, beaded fringe, and instructions for beaded buckles. A revised and simplified the peyote stitch is also illustrated.

Volume Four: In this volume, we introduce an exciting style of beadwork that can be applied to any cross stitch pattern or design. Inlaying beadwork into leather, embroidery with beads, and a helpful hints from the author on business-minded crafters are also included.

Volume Five: In keeping with the demand for new, creative ideas in beading, this volume exposes many time saving short cuts. Each with easy to follow, step by step illustrated instructions. We introduce new techniques in beading and reveal many short cuts and best kept secrets of beading. And of course, there are new and exciting loom patterns and techniques with illustrated instructions. Peggy Sue teaches crocheting with beads and advanced crocheting with beads with lots of new, creative earring fashions.

Volume Six: Volume Six completes the first half of this series. Each volume teaches beadwork and Native American Indian Media, as well as beading fashions of other countries. In Volume 6, we look at designs in tribal identity and its meaning. Quilling and Tambour beading techniques with illustrations are presented as well as, off-loom weaving methods and a new concept on beading. You will enjoy the color sections and new patterns exposed.

Volume Seven: This volumes delves into beadwork patterns and techniques for the nineties through the twenty-first century. Illustrated techniques for cutting your beading time has been revealed, plus new earring techniques and patterns. Peggy Sue gives tips for marketing your craft. Also included: Southwestern history, transposing pictures to bead graph, the lacy daisy weave, conchos, conchos and bead braiding, bead braiding necklaces, double needle cross over, cross needle earring, contemporary bead weaving, beaded boot spats and much more.